COSTUME AND FASHION SOURCE BOOKS

Colonial America

Deirdre Clancy Steer and Amela Baksic

Produced for Chelsea House by Bailey Publishing Associates Ltd, 11a Woodlands, Hove BN3 6TJ, England

Project Manager: Patience Coster
Text Designer: Jane Hawkins
Picture Research: Shelley Noronha
Artist: Deirdre Clancy Steer

Library of Congress Cataloging-in-Publication Data
Steer, Deirdre Clancy.
Colonial America / Deirdre Clancy Steer and Amela Baksic.
p. cm. -- (Costume source books)
Includes bibliographical references and index.
ISBN 978-1-60413-380-6
1. Clothing and dress--United States--History--17th century--Juvenile literature. 2. Clothing and dress--United States--History--18th century--Juvenile literature. 3. United States--Social life and customs--To 1775--Juvenile literature. I. Baksic, Amela. II. Title. III. Series.
GT607.C53 2009
391.009032--dc22
2008047257

Chelsea House books are available at special discounts when purchased in bulk quantities for businesses, associations, institutions, or sales promotions. Please call our Special Sales Department in New York on (212) 967-8800 or (800) 322-8755. You can find Chelsea House on the World Wide Web at: http://www.chelseahouse.com.

Printed and bound in China

CP PKGR 10 9 8 7 6 5 4 3 2 1

The publishers would like to thank the following for permission to reproduce their pictures: Art Archive: 7 (Galerie La Tour Camoufle Louvre des Antiquaires/Gianni Dagli Orti), 11 (National Gallery London/Eileen Tweedy), 25 (Christ's Hospital/Eileen Tweedy), 33 *top* (Museum of Fine Arts Boston/Laurie Platt Winfrey), 35 (Metropolitan Museum of Art New York/Laurie Platt Winfrey), 36 (Musée du Louvre, Paris/Alfredo Dagli Orti); Bailey Publishing Associates Ltd: *contents page*, 13 *top*, 33 *bottom*; Bridgeman Art Library: 8 (© Museum of London, UK), 6 *detail* and 9 (Johnny van Haeften Gallery, London, UK), 16 (Musée des Beaux-Arts, Agen, France/Lauros/Giraudon), 17 (Roy Miles Fine Paintings), 14 *detail* and 18 (© Wallace Collection, London, UK), 19, 24 *detail*, and 44 *detail* (Charlecote Park, Warwickshire, UK/National Trust Photographic Library/Derrick E. Witty), 21 (© Wallace Collection, London, UK), 22 (Hamburger Kunsthalle, Hamburg, Germany), 26 (Private Collection/Photo © Christie's Images), 30 (Private Collection/Photo © Christie's Images), 37 (Brooklyn Museum of Art, New York, USA), 36 *detail* and 42 (Brooklyn Museum of Art, New York, USA/Designated Purchase Fund), 50 (Washington University, St. Louis, USA), 53 (Museum of Fine Arts, Houston, Texas, USA/The Bayou Bend Collection, gift of Miss Ima Hogg), 54 (© The Holburne Museum of Art, Bath, UK), 56 (Private Collection), 58 (The Putnam Foundation, Timken Museum of Art, San Diego, USA), 52 *detail* and 59 *left* (Burrell Collection, Glasgow, Scotland/ © Glasgow City Council, Museums), 59 *right* (© Cheltenham Art Gallery & Museums, Gloucestershire, UK); Corbis: 5 (© Marilyn Angel Wynn/Nativestock Pictures), 10 (© Richard T. Nowitz), 12 (© Bettmann), *title page* and 13 *bottom* (© Museum of the City of New York), 14 (© Farrell Grehan), 24 (© Bettmann), 28 (© Richard T. Nowitz), 29 (© Burstein Collection), 32 (© Lee Snider/Photo Images), 34 (© Robert Holmes), 38 (© Mark E. Gibson), 39 (© Burstein Collection), 40 (© Wolfgang Kaehler), 43 (© Richard T. Nowitz), 46 (© Bob Krist), 51 (© Richard T. Nowitz), 52 (© Brian Snyder/Reuters); Kobal Collection: 45 (20th Century Fox/Morgan Creek/Connor, Frank), 47 (MGM), 48 (Goldcrest-Viking/Warner Bros); Rex Features: 6; TopFoto: 23 (Art Media/HIP), 27 (© 2000 Michael Geissinger/The Image Works), 44 ©Jim Commentucci/Syracuse Newspapers/The Image Works); Victoria and Albert Museum: 20 (© V&A Images), 55 (© V&A Images).

Contents

Introduction

The colonial era in North America started with the founding of Jamestown, Virginia, in 1607 and continued until the American Revolutionary War of 1775–83. In this book, we will refer to colonial Americans as those people who left England, Holland (the Netherlands), and many other European countries during the seventeenth and eighteenth centuries to settle in the original thirteen North American states on the eastern seaboard.

Most of the first settlers at Jamestown were English. They had been sent across the Atlantic by the Virginia Company of London to find treasure (mainly gold and precious minerals) in the New World. Some of these adventurers had money problems back home and didn't intend to return, so they brought everything they could with them on the ships. Their costumes were ordinary Englishmen's wear of the early Jacobean period (1604–15) and included clothes for hunting, riding, light warfare, and, of course, for show. These settlers were followed in 1620 by the *Mayflower* Pilgrims, whose dress and culture were much more sober than those of their forebears. A flood of other European immigrants soon arrived.

Below: In Jamestown, re-enactors take part in a reconstruction of the daily lives of the settlers.

This book will show you how to dress as people did in the colonial era so that you can take part in plays, parades, and other re-enactments. You can dress up as a wealthy adventurer, a modest Pilgrim Mother, a showy New York lady, a periwigged church minister, or a Revolutionary soldier. Finding or customizing fabrics to achieve a contemporary colonial look is very important, as are details such as hats, stockings, shoes, and hairstyles.

A PILGRIM'S WARDROBE

"The general opinion was that the Pilgrims were pretty badly off in the way of clothing, &c. so Pastor Virgin read an inventory of the wardrobe of Elder Brewster, who came over in the *Mayflower*. This document showed that the worldly Elder was the happy possessor of 8 pairs of stockings, 5 waistcoats, 3 suits of underclothes—one suit made of leather—2 gowns, 4 cloth suits, 2 black coats, 2 pairs of trousers, 1 cloak, 1 doublet, 2 belts, 2 pairs of gloves, 2 hats, 36 handkerchiefs, 8 capes, 7 bands, 1 pair of gaiters and 1 violet-colored coat. The inventory also included a pistol, a dagger, 2 knives, a rapier, two swords, a tobacco case, a tobacco box and . . . sundry pipes. Altogether Elder Brewster was pretty well fixed."

An article in the *New York Times*, December 23, 1884, describes the *Mayflower* colonists

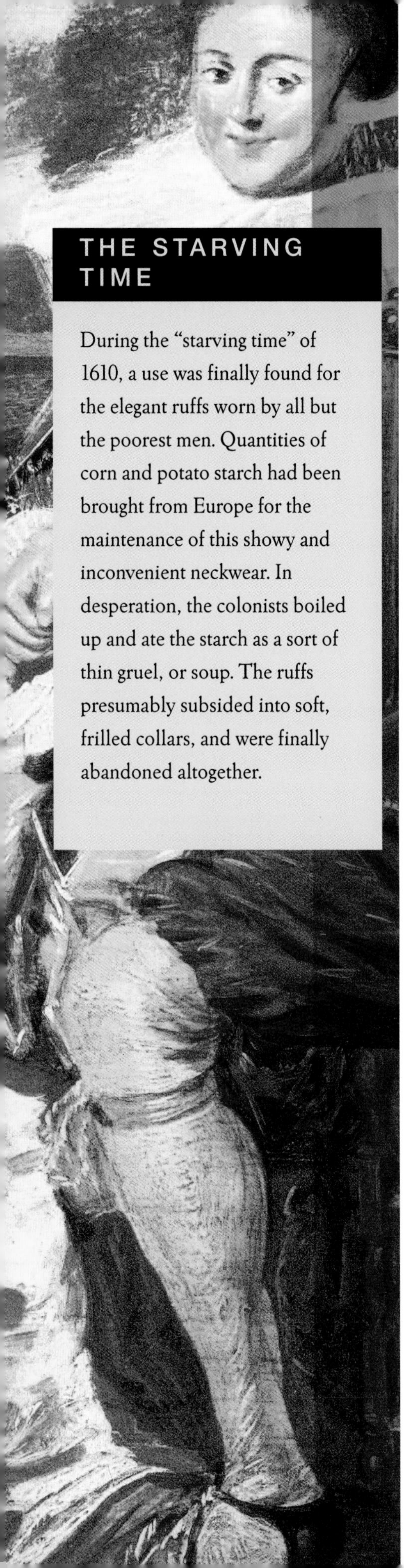

CHAPTER 1

The First Settlers

THE STARVING TIME

During the "starving time" of 1610, a use was finally found for the elegant ruffs worn by all but the poorest men. Quantities of corn and potato starch had been brought from Europe for the maintenance of this showy and inconvenient neckwear. In desperation, the colonists boiled up and ate the starch as a sort of thin gruel, or soup. The ruffs presumably subsided into soft, frilled collars, and were finally abandoned altogether.

THE MEN ARRIVE

In the 1500s, European explorers made several forays into North America. The French, who first arrived in 1534, occupied lands that included Louisiana and Quebec. The Spanish held huge territories in the West that extended all the way to Alaska.

The passengers on the English ships landing in 1607 at Jamestown, a site on a river near Chesapeake Bay, were all male. Many of them were adventurers who had been lured to the New World by stories of riches and easy financial reward. At least half of them had been brought up to be "gentlemen," and the last thing they expected was to have to do hard, physical work. Apart from an ability to issue orders, most of them had no useful survival skills, and they knew very little about how to work for a living. Nevertheless, some of the gentlemen, and certainly many of the craftsmen and laborers who accompanied them, made every effort to ensure the colony succeeded. Humble domestic activities, such as cooking, sewing, mending, and washing, were carried out by women or

Above: English explorers venture into uncharted waters as they make their way up the river to colonize Jamestown in the 2005 movie *The New World*.

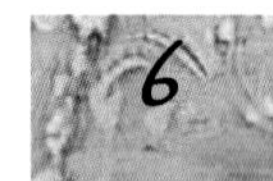

Right: European soldiers wore an open-faced helmet and a cuirass (breast and back plates). This armor gave them some protection from the spears and arrows of the Native Americans.

servants who arrived later. Heavier outdoor jobs, such as farming, carpentry, glass making, and house building, were undertaken by craftsmen and other working people.

The early years in colonial America were tough. Half of the arrivals in Jamestown died from disease and starvation during the first severe winter. Other setbacks included wars with the Native American population and another freezing winter known as the "starving time" of 1610, during which only 60 of the original 214 settlers survived. Several fires also destroyed the hastily constructed wooden buildings, along with most of the colonists' clothes. However, despite the threat of malarial mosquitoes in summer and bitter cold in winter, the tiny outpost in Virginia battled on. Its people traded for food with the local Native American people and eventually began to start growing and trading in a lucrative new cash crop—tobacco. In 1614, the first shipment of Virginia tobacco was sold in London.

MEN'S WEAR

At the start of the seventeenth century, a man's suit of clothes consisted of a doublet, breeches, and a cape, or casaque. This suit was worn over a linen long-tailed shirt and linen underpants and accessorized with stockings, shoes or boots, a hat, and, if the man was wealthy, gloves.

The doublet had been the main male upper body garment since the Middle Ages. Doublets were much the same shape as a modern jean jacket but were longer in the waist and had more padding. They had evolved from comfortable jackets worn under armor or for fencing practice, so they were always tight-fitting and interlined with stitched, padded linen. The sleeves were often detachable and made from a softer fabric. They were cut with a curve to fit the bent elbow and had

ARMOR

Soldiers were armed with a harquebus (a portable, long-barreled gun), a sword, and a pair of pistols. Helmets were lined with a quilted cap to cushion the head. A heavy, buff leather coat was worn under the armor for added protection.

Right: This man's leather doublet shows the tight-fitting style that was popular in the early 1600s.

A COLORFUL END

Starch was usually made from boiled corn or potatoes. It came in a range of colors: plain white, pale blue (from rice flour), and a sunny yellow (from saffron). This yellow starch was apparently invented by a certain Miss Turner, who, though ultra-fashionable, was beheaded for poisoning a lord. At her execution, all in attendance, including the axman, wore large, saffron-colored ruffs in her honor. However, perhaps nervous about the association with Miss Turner, no one wore yellow ruffs thereafter.

epaulettes (small shoulder pieces). The basque, or flared band under the waist seam, was cut into tabs. The lower stomach had yet more padding, or "belly pieces," to stiffen the front.

TRUNK HOSE

At the beginning of the seventeenth century, breeches were very short and wide and called trunk hose. They were padded with straw and horsehair and finished with tight thigh bands, called canions. By 1615, breeches had become much longer and less padded, but they were still cut very full and finished with a narrow band at the knee. Until about 1620, the breeches were laced to the waistband of the doublet using tags visible from the outside; later, hooks sewn to the inside of the waistband were used. The breeches were usually interlined with a wool material and lined with linen cut straight to hold the baggy outer shape in place. They must have been very cozy and warm in winter, and unpleasantly hot and scratchy in the mosquito-ridden Virginia summer.

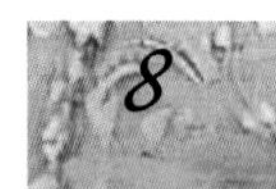

Above: In this seventeenth-century Dutch painting, the ruff worn by the woman in the center is of extravagant and impractical proportions.

THE WOMEN ARRIVE

The first women to land in Jamestown were Mistress Forrester and her maid, Anne Barras, in 1608. Soon, however, it became apparent that more women were needed to stabilize the colony. Without them, many of the men would simply stay for a couple of years to make as much money as they could, then return to England. The Virginia Company therefore began to recruit young, active women. The men were much less likely to sail home if their wives and children were with them in America.

Most of the first women of Jamestown were workers rather than grand ladies. Many of them arrived as indentured servants, which means they paid off the cost of their passage with seven years of hard work. At the end of this time, they received a share in some land and an almost guaranteed husband, since the ratio of men to women was six to one for many years. However, the Virginia Company arranged that, if a man could afford it, he could send an order for a better class of woman since it was unacceptable to marry across the rigid class divide.

THE RICH AND THEIR RUFFS

Ruffs came into fashion in the mid-sixteenth century and steadily grew larger and more elaborate. Queen Elizabeth I even passed laws to try to restrict their size, but without success. By the end of the sixteenth century, women's ruffs had become so large that the wearer needed an especially long spoon to reach her mouth while eating.

The largest ruffs were extremely expensive to make, using as much as 7 yards (6 meters) of cloth and requiring up to 600 pleats. Special small-size ruffs were also worn around the wrists as cuffs. Clearly, ruffs were a luxury item that only the wealthy people in society could afford. They were also very time-consuming to prepare and wash. The rigid appearance of the ruff was maintained by soaking it in a hot starch solution, then, using cone-shaped pegs, working it into shape while still damp. The ruff was then baked in a cool oven for several hours until dry.

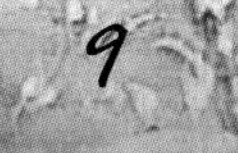

Right: A woman in period costume cooks outdoors at the Jamestown historical site.

COLORS

Everyday clothes were made with fabrics of many colors. All shades of brown were used, from bright brick and russet to the darkest mulberry, and red dye was made from madder roots. Yellow and soft blue dyes from woad and indigo were popular, as were gentle greens. Other garments were made of cloth that wasn't dyed at all. These clothes were gray, brown, or white, the natural color of the cloth. They were made from unbleached linen, which is a brown-paper-envelope color, or brown wool from old breeds of sheep.

It wasn't easy to achieve the solid, long-lasting black that was so much in demand for formal garments. Black was a difficult dye to work with—one recipe involved iron oxide, which is sometimes derived from rusty nails or steel wool and vinegar, and is often used to dye leather. Another recipe used oak gall. Depending on the recipe, black garments tended to fade to a strange mildewed green with age or, with exposure to sunlight, to a rusty brown.

In the first part of the seventeenth century, girls and women wore a linen chemise, or undersmock. This was white or natural in color so that it would survive vigorous washing. The garment had a round neck with a drawstring and square-cut sleeves. It was knee length or a little longer and was seldom removed since very few women wore, or even possessed, separate nightgowns. Underpants or drawers were not worn because they were considered indecent.

A rigidly boned corset was worn over the chemise. Two petticoats, or underskirts, were worn and were held out from the lower body by

a padded hip roll (known as a bum roll). A long, full, gathered, or cartridge-pleated skirt went over the top of these. A tight-sleeved bodice fastened in front with metal hooks and bars or with laces in the two seams that shaped the back of the garment. For a while in the 1600s, women could leave their corsets off because the boning was built into the bodice—sandwiched between the interlining and the lining. However, this fashion did not last long.

Lower-class women such as Anne Barras wore a warm cloak, together with knitted or bias-cut wool hose held up with garters and sturdy leather shoes with low-stacked heels. The hair was wound in a bun and covered at all times by a linen cap topped, when the woman was out of doors or in church, by a black felt hat.

Mistress Forrester's garments were made from far richer, more colorful fabrics, with decoration, such as ribbons, embroidery, and pinked slashes. Her jacket was fastened with ribbons, and she wore a large starched ruff on formal occasions. A long over-gown with open hanging sleeves was a popular choice; this was either fitted and buttoned to the neck or loose and open with the bodice showing underneath. The mistress's hair was dressed and curled with hot tongs, the back hair fixed in a small bun and the side hair fluffed out like a spaniel's ears.

Above: This Dutch painting of ordinary seventeenth-century life shows an assortment of women's costume. The middle-class housewife choosing fish from a market stall wears a warm fur-trimmed jacket, or samare. Her skirts are protected by a clean white linen apron. The working-class "fishwife" wears a red flannel bodice over her chemise, a black overall apron, and what looks like a man's black pull-on hat.

Above: A male settler signs the Mayflower Compact, a document that set out the first laws for the new land. In the background, the womenfolk tend to their traditional activities of Bible-reading, baby-minding, and sewing.

PAID-FOR WOMEN

The male colonists bought many of the first women in Jamestown with 150 pounds of the best tobacco leaf. These paid-for women began their lives in the colony with clothing and bedding provided by the Virginia Company, including a petticoat, a waistcoat, stockings, garters, smocks, gloves, a hat, an apron, two pairs of shoes, a towel, two head coifs, a pair of sheets, and a rug.

Sometimes small, curled bangs were worn. It's hard to imagine how a woman managed to keep up this standard of hairdressing on board the cramped ship from England and during the early days of the colony!

PILGRIMS

In the winter of 1620, the ship the *Mayflower* arrived in Plymouth, Massachusetts, after crossing the Atlantic from Southampton, England. The people on board were very different from the adventurers of Jamestown. The dominant group was made up of Separatists, who wanted to separate from the Church of England and form independent churches. Also aboard the Mayflower were "Strangers," a group made up largely of craftsmen and yeoman farmers from East Anglia in England, who had been recruited to help establish the new colony.

Although they weren't grand or rich, the Pilgrims had advantages over the first colonists, who settled farther south. The men had brought their wives and children with them, which gave stability to the group. Because of their class and temperament, the Pilgrims believed in the virtue of hard work. They were true Christian fundamentalists, meaning that everything they did, from the way they dressed and wore their hair to how they organized themselves as a community, was prescribed by the Bible, particularly the Old Testament. Even in the United States today, the Old Order Amish communities live by a similar dress code, for the same reasons.

THE IMPORTANCE OF BLACK

In many portraits of that time, people are shown wearing black, and the popular image of the Pilgrims is that they all wore it. However, ordinary folk probably wore less black than we imagine, for two reasons. First, only grand people had their pictures painted, and second, the sitters liked to wear their best clothes for their portraits, and those clothes, in the 1620s, were usually black. Nevertheless, black was certainly favored by important people in the community. Church ministers, governors, and judges wore it as a uniform to emphasize their seriousness and authority.

Right: Simple collars replaced impractical ruffs in the Plymouth colony. *Below:* This nineteenth-century painting shows the *Mayflower* Pilgrims landing at Plymouth, Massachusetts, in December 1620.

A LADY'S WARDROBE

"One petticoat, scarlet
One striped stuff petticoat with black lace
Two colored drugget [wool] petticoats with gray linings
Two colored drugget petticoats with white linings
One colored drugget petticoat with pointed lace
One black silk petticoat with ash gray silk lining . . .
One black silk crape samare with tucker
Three flowered calico samares
Three calico nightgowns, one flowered, two red
One silk waistcoat, one calico waistcoat
One pair of bodices
Five pair white cotton stocking
Three black love hoods [light headscarf-like hoods] . . .
Two pair sleeves with great lace . . .
One black silk rain cloth cap
One black plush mask"

A wealthy woman's clothing list from 1662

CHAPTER 2

Costume in the Colonies

BIRTH OF THE SUIT

By 1620, the doublet and short breeches had been abandoned and men wore a suit of garments made from wool or leather, with a wool cloak. The coat replaced the doublet, with much of the padding and interfacing discarded to make a softer line. The little tabs of the basque became just four pieces, two at the front and two at the back, and lengthened to mid-thigh, a useful jacket length. Sleeves, which had developed from the casaque, were still open along the front seam with many buttons, showing the full-sleeved shirt beneath. The ruff collapsed, lost its fullness, and became a simple linen or lace collar, tied with a small tasseled cord. Breeches were full and baggy, fastening just below the knee.

Women's clothing followed a changing silhouette similar to that of the men, with an even greater difference between the grand ladies and the plain dress used by the Pilgrim Mothers (the name given to the women

Above: Actors dressed as settlers at a living history museum of Pilgrim life. Note the split sleeve of the man's coat, showing the shirt beneath.

A young colonial couple, around 1620
Large hat of stiffened, felted wool
Long hair, beard, and mustache
Square-cut cream linen shirt with a large collar
Fitted wool doublet lined with linen
Thick cowhide or buff jerkin worn over the doublet
Full breeches, pleated into the waist and gathered into bands above the knee
Hand-knitted hose
Square-toed, thigh-length leather boots, worn turned down
White linen cap over center-parted hair pulled back into a bun
White linen collar
Simple gray wool bodice worn over a corset stiffened with steel, whalebone, or stiff grasses
Gray wool skirt, here worn hitched up for ease of movement
Linen apron
Red flannel petticoat
Low-heeled tongue-and-buckle shoes

Right: This seventeenth-century portrait shows an aristocratic young lady in a soft chemise, with a jeweled, armor-like, waist-cinching corset. Her hair, left uncovered, is teased into "kiss curls" on her forehead.

who arrived on the *Mayflower*). As with men, the ruff collapsed, softened, and was soon replaced completely by a collar or triangular scarf called a fichu.

Alternatively, for grand ladies a wide lace trim over the top of the bodice became the new style. Fashionable women wore their hair longer, and some very daring ladies wore their hair uncovered. Waists were raised with a straight-fronted corset that came to a point at the waistline. Sleeves became much fuller and were slashed into panes to show the chemise beneath.

CLEANLINESS IS NEXT TO GODLINESS

The Pilgrim Mothers prided themselves on the perfect whiteness of their linen and made their own soap from lye (the ashes from the fire) or from the barilla plant, which was boiled and mixed with tallow (animal fat).

THE PILGRIM MOTHERS

The everyday costume of the Pilgrim Mothers consisted of a simple bodice with sleeves of medium fullness worn over a chemise and boned corset or under-bodice. The skirt was worn over one or two petticoats, a bum roll, home-knitted hose held up with garters, and square-toed, tongue-and-buckle leather shoes. A white fichu or plain collar and cuffs were always worn, as was an apron. Women and girls wore a small white cap over their hair at all times, even in the house, and a tall-brimmed black hat when out of doors. A jacket fitted to the waist—with a flared basque and half-length sleeves—could be added for warmth, and women wore a long cloak with a hood when outdoors. Red, heavily milled wool was a popular choice, even among Puritans.

If you are making a Pilgrim costume, the correct fabric is linen for the white items and wool of various weights for everything else. A popular mixture at the time was linsey-woolsey, a fabric with a linen warp and a wool weft. This would be perfect for re-enactment purposes, but it's hard to find today. Seventeenth-century wool fabric was much stiffer and more tightly woven than it is now. A convincing replacement is wool mixed with silk (beautiful but pricey) or heavy cotton. Furnishing-weight cotton fabric or cotton mixed with linen will work, as will moleskin cotton.

SOAP-MAKING—AN EVEN OLDER WAY

Soapwort (*Saponaria officinalis*) is a common perennial plant from the carnation family. The scientific name *Saponaria* is derived from the Latin *sapo*, meaning "soap," which, like its common name, refers to its cleaning properties. Soapwort produces lather when brought into contact with water and has been used as a gentle wool wash for centuries. Swiss farmers sometimes use it to shampoo their sheep before shearing. A solution of soapwort can be used to wash precious antique textiles and as a shampoo.

Below: A Puritan family group, dressed in severe black and white. The only touch of color is the pale pink of the younger woman's underskirt. Note that the parent couple wear old-fashioned starched ruffs, while the young people sport the new, lace-trimmed falling collars.

Above: This wonderful Dutch "slice of life" painting is full of valuable costume details. Surrounded by women, the father has been left "holding the baby." The only other man present is sloping away, with a pitying smirk on his face.

MAKE IT— A CORSET

You can make a corset from a tightly woven cotton or linen fabric. Cut the fabric to shape from one of the many patterns available. Stitch the long seams and the channels. Check the fit, since it's difficult to change it once the bones are in place. Bind the lower edges. Hammer in the eyelets. Use steel or plastic boning or, for a really authentic peasant costume, bunches of thin, dried reeds. Bind the top edge and insert the laces. You should be able to reduce your waist measurement by up to 4 inches (10 centimeters) by wearing a corset.

THE COLORFUL DUTCH

While the New Englanders were governed by Puritan traditions, the Dutch settlers who arrived in New Amsterdam (New York, as it became) in 1613 had a more laid-back approach to life. They enjoyed dancing and music-making, and their general outlook was reflected in more colorful clothes. Brightly colored petticoats were short enough to reveal green and blue stockings embroidered with "clocks." Skirts and bodices were red, yellow, or blue, and the typical Dutch jacket was a sunny yellow, trimmed with white fur. Dutch merchants preferred to wear black, but young men also liked to wear garments that were brighter than the "sad" (meaning dark or thoughtful) colors of New England.

CHILDREN

Newborn babies were automatically wrapped in swaddling clothes or bands, believed to help the limbs grow straight. Baby dresses were either simple sack-shaped garments drawn in at the neck with a narrow cord or little straight-waisted gowns like those of their parents. All were handmade with tiny stitches—one stitch to every four threads was the rule. Wool petticoats seem not to have been used. Instead, the underclothes were of linen or some fine fabric such as cotton dimity. Little shawls around the shoulders provided warmth; the shawls were often crossed in front and tied in a knot at the back. Once the baby could walk, it was dressed in an apron called a pinner or pinafore, so named because the bib was pinned on before (in front). The baby wore a "pudding," or pudding cap, on its head. This looked rather like a football helmet but was made of cloth stuffed with soft wool or linen shreds. It acted as a head guard in case the toddler fell or knocked its head.

Little girls were dressed as small replicas of their mothers, even to the extent that they sometimes wore lightweight corsets called "jumps." Until they reached the age of five or six, boys were dressed like girls, except that their dresses had a more coat-like form. A big day for any small boy was when his first suit of real grown-up clothes was measured, made, and finally put on. The whole family gathered round to admire the new "little man."

Below: This portrait of the Lucy family, from 1630, is full of lovely details, both of costume and home life. The three older girls are dressed in almost identical fine gowns. The three younger children are boys still dressed as girls. The young man entering on the left of the painting, bearing fruit, is probably a page boy.

KNITTING STOCKINGS

Circular knitting, also known as knitting in the round, is a form of construction that creates a seamless tube. The garment is worked in rounds (the equivalent of rows in flat knitting) in a spiral. Traditionally, circular knitting is done using a set of four or five double-pointed needles and is employed to create tube-shaped pieces such as hats, stockings, mittens, and sleeves. Knitting stockings takes skill. The difficult part is when the knitter "turns the heel" by extending half the tube on two of the needles to fit the bulge of the heel. The knitter then joins the work up again with the front of the stocking, which has been held on the other two needles.

TUNEFUL KNITTING

"There a young shepherdess knitting and withal singing, and it seemed that her voice comforted her hands to work and her hands kept time to her voice's music."

Sir Philip Sydney, *Arcadia* (1577)

KNITTED GARMENTS

In certain parts of England, during the seventeenth century, knitting was a common occupation of poorer people, for whom it was an important source of income. Girls and women knitted stockings all year round; men joined in between the harvest in September and the start of the lambing season in February. They would make stockings and caps for the family's use and sell the rest. After all, everyone needed hose, which even with careful darning wore out rather quickly. Norfolk was a knitting center, and it was the home county of many of the first arrivals to New England, who brought their skills, and their needles, with them.

It's likely that knitting was far more common in the early days of the colonies than is usually supposed. It was such a simple domestic thing to do, requiring only basic equipment. To knit a garment, a person would need spun yarn and two or four easily made wood or bone needles. Unlike other forms of garment-making, knitting required no highly taxed imported cloth. Knitted caps and felted hats and undershirts were all made, but the most time-consuming task was the knitting of the many pairs of stockings needed by each family. New England winters were cold and long, far harsher than in damp England, so a knitted undershirt or a soft house jacket would have been very welcome.

LACE

The tradition of lace-making was known in England from 1563. The craft was brought to colonial America by English, Dutch, and Irish lace makers. Like knitting, lace-making was a good occupation to while away

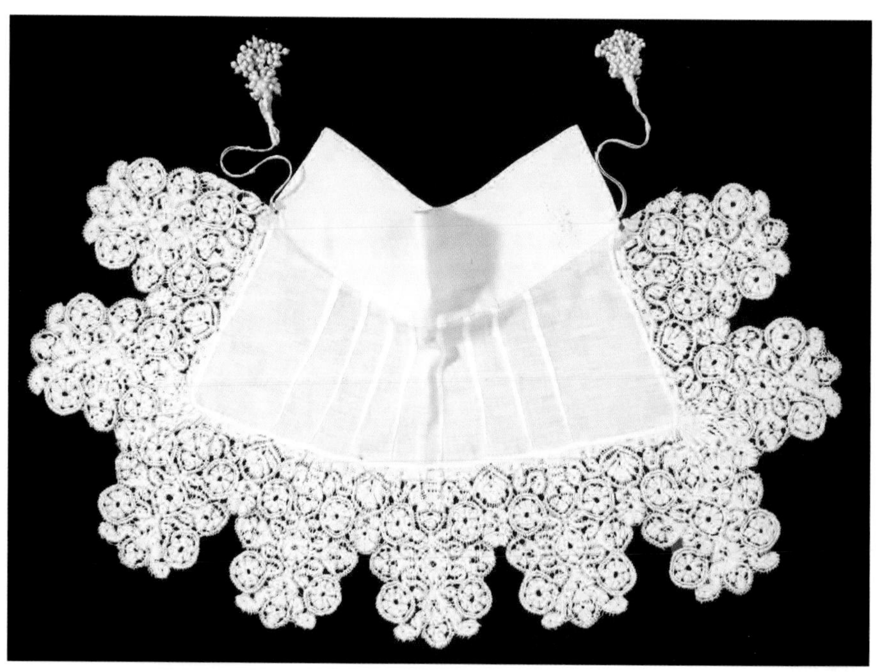

Right: This man's collar is made of fine linen, edged with bobbin lace, and decorated with tassels of knotted thread.

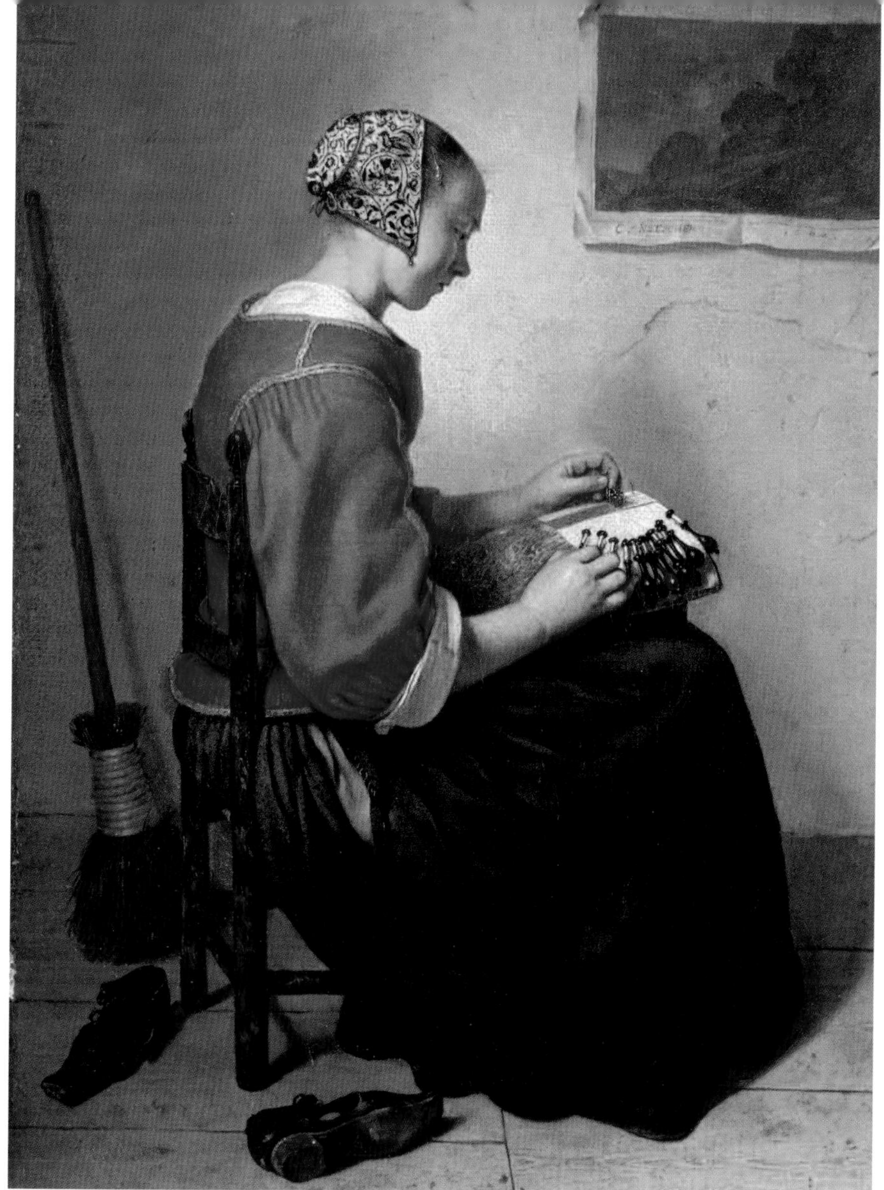

THE LACE MAKERS

Women would sit outside their homes in daylight, with the lace attached to a pillow resting on a stool (called a pillow horse). Colorful bobbins holding threads would be twisted around pins in perforated parchment bearing the pattern for the old point lace. The pins had probably been made by the local pin maker. Originally, bobbins were made of bone, but later, wood bobbins were used.

Left: This young woman, demurely occupied at the making of bobbin, or pillow lace, wears a little linen cap, embroidered in black work. She is also wearing a cheerful red bodice over her chemise and a black skirt, in which you can see the split for a pocket. She has kicked off her well-worn black shoes.

the hours once the heavy work was finished, and it was often done in groups who sang to help the rhythm of the bobbins along. Fine lace was imported from England, where it was made by poorly paid home workers, but the craft was also practiced in colonial America. It was in every sense a cottage industry—a trade generated and sustained by women and girls working in their own homes to earn a meager amount of money. Even men became lace makers when work was scarce after the harvest.

BOOTS, SHOES, CLOGS, AND PATTENS

The one extravagance the seventeenth-century colonial man could not give up was that of his tremendous boots. They were built of thick coach-hide with square toes, stacked heels, and knee guards that reached the thigh. Literally "as tough as old boots," they could last

JACKBOOTS

Military boots were known as jackboots. This was because they were dyed with black dye made from iron oxide (rusty nails or steel wool) and vinegar. The same dye was used to stain leather drinking bottles, or "jacks," and gave rise to the French comment that "English men drank from their boots."

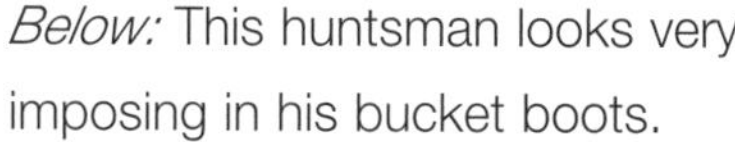

for generations. Frugal folk complained about their use because they took as much leather to make as six pairs of ordinary shoes.

The thigh-high boots of the Elizabethan era had clothed and protected the legs in a dramatic way when breeches were very short. But these boots went out of fashion as breeches got longer. Soldiers, or those who wished to be thought of as very manly, still wore the boots but pushed them down so that they wrinkled. They then turned over the top half either with one fold or down and up again to form the bucket boot. The turnovers were decorated with boot cuffs, which were sometimes simple cloth liners. These protected the man's expensive knitted hose from wear against the tough leather. At other times, they were made from decorative lace that probably didn't provide any protection but looked very fine.

Women of "the lower orders" might have worn sensible shoes with thick, durable soles, but no "lady" did. Upper- and middle-class women always wore shoes of lightweight kid or brocade, with medium-to-high shaped heels and thin leather soles. They were as fragile as they looked. Wealthy women did not walk far; instead, they usually rode pillion, or

Below: This huntsman looks very imposing in his bucket boots.

Left: The woman in this painting is eating oysters prepared and offered to her by a group of men, while revealing her dainty shoes in a casual manner. Such decadent behavior would have been frowned on by her Puritan contemporaries.

on a light saddle, behind their husband or servant. When they did take a long walk, overshoes came to the rescue. These were of two main types: pattens and clogs. Pattens were made to lift the wearer above the dirt of the streets. A steel hoop was fixed to the carved wooden sole, and the leather uppers were open at the heel so that the lady could slip her foot, with its delicate indoor shoe, into the patten. Clogs had no steel lift but were carved directly out of wood, with leather uppers fixed in place with small nails. Children and millworkers sometimes wore clogs on their own, without indoor shoes.

All this weather footwear made a tremendous noise: a group of ladies so dressed clattered over the cobbled streets like a herd of ponies. Not surprisingly, it was forbidden to wear overshoes in church—they had to be left neatly in the church porch. Pattens and clogs also made women walk with a strange, tripping sort of trot, much like Japanese ladies in their split-toed platform shoes.

SHOE WARNING

Heavy-soled shoes were unknown for women's wear. The fashion for delicate shoes meant that women wore clogs constantly to protect their footwear in America's unpaved streets. Among the Pilgrims, however, fancy shoes were frowned on. A letter of instruction to Quaker women, written in 1720, warned them not to wear: "Shoes of light Colours bound with Differing Colours, and heels White or Red, with White bands, and fine Coloured Clogs and Strings, and Scarlet and Purple Stockings and Petticoats made Short to expose them." Again, in 1726, in Burlington, New Jersey, Quakers were asked to be "careful to avoid wearing of Stript Shoos, or Red and White Heel'd Shoos, or Clogs, or Shoos trimmed with Gawdy Colours."

STYLE TIP

The periwig and other similar types of wig pose endless problems for the actor or re-enactor. Where possible, it's often better to use a cap of some kind, either embroidered or wool, depending on the class of person being represented. Nylon wigs can be used if it's necessary to have a periwig, but these are far too shiny and skimpy for full-bottomed wigs, and the white wigs are far too bright. You can make periwigs look good on stage by simply using two at a time to increase the fullness and length. Spray with dulling spray. For a more convincing white or gray wig, spray lightly with hair lacquer and powder with flour or fuller's earth.

CHAPTER 3

Growth

THE COLONISTS PROSPER

In the 1630s and 1640s, at least 20,000 people immigrated to the New England area. They were mostly yeoman families, and these industrious people made a great success of their new life, working as farmers, hunters, and craftspeople of all kinds. As the seventeenth century progressed, the colonies grew in size and number, and European culture, clothing, and habits spread across the region. Not long after the Pilgrims arrived in Plymouth, the Puritans came to Massachusetts and settled Naumkeag (later called Salem). In 1630, they founded the city of Boston. In 1664, the Dutch surrendered to English forces and New Amsterdam was given to King Charles II's brother, the duke of York, and renamed New York.

Above: At a re-enactment of the first Thanksgiving, the Pilgrims bless their food and give thanks to God for their successful harvest.

PECULIAR FASHIONS

Back home in England, the male fashions of the court had become quite peculiar. The coat grew increasingly shorter in the sleeves and body, and the breeches grew very wide and were open at the knee. As diarist Samuel Pepys reported: "Mr Townsend put both legs through one knee of his breeches, and so went all day." A mania for ribbon meant that over a hundred yards could be used to decorate one outfit. Waistbands, sleeves, shoulders, and breeches were garlanded with bows, loops, and rosettes in a rainbow of colors. The front of the shirt collar was decorated with a cravat of handmade lace and finished with yet another ribbon bow. Colonial men of high rank refused to wear the feminine frills and ribbons of the British and French courts. Therefore, when visiting sea captains went swaggering through the streets of still-Puritan, soberly dressed Boston, they must have met with disapproving stares.

AN INCONVENIENT FASHION

In 1660s Europe, men of fashion started to wear wigs. A fashion for enormous, curled, spaniel-eared periwigs started, it is said, when King Louis XIV of France went bald at the age of twenty-three. The entire French aristocracy donned wigs out of well-bred sympathy. This expensive, high-maintenance, unhygienic, and inconvenient fashion continued to be worn by almost all men, at least on formal occasions, for the next 170 years.

Wigs were made from various hairy materials, but the most sought after was human hair. This was sometimes cut from the head of the wig wearer himself. On other occasions, it was the hair of nuns, who shaved their heads as they took vows of poverty, chastity, and obedience. Rumor has it that the corpses of those unfortunates who had died of the plague were also shaved to supply the wig trade.

Lawyers' and church ministers' wigs were often made from horsehair taken from the tails of gray and white horses, or from goat hair, shredded hemp, or wool from the coarser-coated breeds of sheep. A popular style of wig—favored by doctors of divinity—with its bulging sides and dangling tail, looked very much like the rear end of a sheep. American

Below: Here Charles II of England is in full ceremonial gear. He wears a tremendous silk-lined, velvet cloak, swirling in deep folds. His full, lace-trimmed linen shirt has a lace cravat tied in a large bow. It is worn with old-fashioned slashed and padded breeches, a red, ermine-trimmed calf-length coat, and high-heeled be-ribboned shoes. The ensemble is finished with a long, dark periwig.

A FINE LIST

"11 new shirts, 4 pair laced sleeves, 8 plane cravats, 4 cravats with lace, 4 striped waistcoats with black buttons, 1 flowered waistcoat, 4 new osenbrig breeches, 1 grey hat with a blew ribbon, 1 dousin black buttons, 3 pair gold buttons, 3 pair silver buttons, 2 pair fine blew stockings, 1 pair fine red stockings, 4 white handkerchiefs, 2 speckled handkerchiefs, 5 pair gloves, 1 stuff coat with black buttons, 1 cloth coat, 1 pair blew plush breeches, 1 pair serge breeches, 2 combs, 1 pair new shoes, silk and thread to mend his clothes."

The wardrobe list of a ten-year-old boy, sent from New York to school in New England at the end of the seventeenth century

men enthusiastically took to the periwig and its many other forms, despite furious grumblings about the "nourishing and frizzling of hair" from some of the particularly devout members of the community.

FASHION RULING

In 1666, King Charles II, perhaps in response to the death toll caused by the Great Fire of London and the decimation of the population by plague, put a stop to some of this silliness. He followed the example of Louis XIV and introduced a sort of uniform to the court, a recognizable suit of clothes that was, with variations, what men wore until the nineteenth century. He decreed that all men should wear a long knee-length coat with cuffs, a vest or waistcoat, and breeches gathered at the waist and knee. They were also required to wear the periwig. High-heeled shoes, with the heels often painted in red, were worn, and a big hat was pulled on over the wig when men went outdoors. The suit was often black, lined with white, which, according to one commentator, made the men look like so many magpies.

Right: Sir Jonathan Trelawny, the bishop of Bristol, Exeter, and Winchester, neatly combines spiritual and worldly power. He wears a black ecclesiastical cassock and an enormous ceremonial velvet robe lined with stiff silk, with ribbons on the shoulders. Around his neck is a simple stock with the linen tabs, or bands, favored by both lawyers and churchmen.

CRAVATS

The collarless coat came into fashion and the ruff was discarded. Instead, neck cloths called cravats were worn. A strip of material about 12 inches (31 centimeters) wide was wrapped around the neck from the front and crossed at the nape at the back; it was then brought to the front again and knotted or tied with a narrow ribbon. By 1792, the cravat was being worn in a more relaxed style, with the long end tucked into the sixth button of the jacket.

Ministers of church and state wore long black robes with white collars, bands, or cravats. These garments were based on the Tudor gown, or houppelande. They had wide sleeves and full backs caught into the armholes and the back yoke with cartridge pleats. The robe was worn over a waistcoat and breeches of black cloth, with black stockings and shoes. Many ministers started wearing large horsehair wigs, a custom that survives in the courts of law in England to this day.

By 1700, the colonist population of America had reached a quarter of a million. The eastern ports, such as Charleston and Philadelphia, were busy trading posts. Here bales of cloth and supplies of equipment, shoes, stockings, sewing tools, and finished garments that had been ordered

Above: Re-enactors portray men of political influence in late-seventeenth-century America. Looking businesslike in knee-length coats and periwigs, they are standing outside the governor's palace in the historic area of Colonial Williamsburg in Virginia.

Right: A wigmaker in Colonial Williamsburg demonstrates her craft. Wigmakers used nails to attach a close-fitting cap of ribbon and cotton or silk net securely to the blockhead. Rows of hair were attached to the cap with a simple, straight stitch. When all the rows of hair were in place, the wigmaker curled them using clay rods.

MADE TO LAST

Eighteenth-century silk gowns were often not perfectly finished inside because they were expected to be altered and remodeled for many years and were often passed from one generation to another. In contrast, shifts, shirts, and other linens, which were worn next to the skin and needed to survive daily washing, were often carefully constructed, with very fine stitches.

when the ship was last in port were exchanged for great quantities of furs, timber, tobacco, raw wool, and even herbs such as sage and ginseng. Shopkeepers and craftsmen—shipwrights, butchers, coopers (barrel makers), seamstresses, tailors, wigmakers, shoemakers, leather workers, bakers, carpenters, masons, and many other specialized producers—made up the middle ranks of society. Wives and husbands often worked together and passed on their craft to their children, who would be expected to help out from an early age.

FASHIONABLE WOMEN ABOUT TOWN

While working and Puritan women wore similar clothes to their mothers' and grandmothers', many more women now had the time and money to follow European fashion with great eagerness. After the rigid gowns of the early 1600s, fashionable ladies' clothing became softer and less straight up and down. Dresses had a higher waist (although this became

Right: This late-seventeenth-century portrait of the wife of a wealthy Boston merchant provides a rare insight into American costume of the time.

lower again after 1670) with puffed elbow-length sleeves that were slashed or simply made of panes (lined strips) to show the full lace-trimmed sleeves of the chemise underneath. This virago sleeve can be seen in almost every portrait of American ladies of the time. It could be caught into as many as five "puffs," with each section held in and decorated with ribbon bows or rosettes. The sleeves were often lined in silk to match the quilted petticoat.

Necklines were low, straight, and trimmed with a deep lace collar, which exposed the shoulders and a little cleavage (since the breasts were now pushed up by the boned corset). The long skirt could be hitched up for walking and to show the gaily colored petticoat, which was often richly embroidered or quilted. Underneath were bright silk stockings and high-heeled shoes, which were tongue-and-buckled with a curved heel.

The pretty petticoat was sometimes worn as a skirt with a samare, or jacket. These useful garments were much favored by Dutch women but

THE WOMEN OF NEW YORK

"Their hair, untortured by the abominations of art, was scrupulously pomatumed back from their foreheads with a candle, and covered with a little cap of quilted calico, which fitted exactly to their heads. Their petticoats of linsey-woolsey were striped with a variety of gorgeous dyes, though I must confess those gallant garments were rather short, scarce reaching below the knee; but then they made up in the number, which generally equaled that of the gentlemen's small-clothes; and what is still more praise-worthy, they were all of their own manufacture, of which circumstance, as may well be supposed, they were not a little vain."

A contemporary account of the Dutch women of New York

Right: This unusual portrait shows a woman wearing a fur-trimmed, velvet samare over her silk dress. She is posing against an Eastern background and is wearing a headdress modeled on the turban.

COATS

In 1660, coats were cut straight and collarless, but during the 1690s, the skirts of coats increased in volume, with the fullness springing from the hips. The cuffs were large and turned back and held in place with buttons. The best fabric to use is something so tightly woven that it can simply be cut and stitched since no turned hem will look as smart or as accurate. Boiled wool is a good choice. Leather, suede, non-woven suede cloth, or even felt are also excellent. If you're worried about the coat fraying, stitch close to the edge or spray with fabric adhesive.

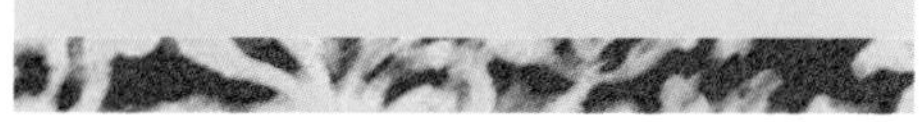

STYLE TIP

Eye masks were popular with ladies in the colonies. Masks made of black silk and velvet were worn in the winter, and green masks were popular in the summer.

were also worn by many others. They were essentially a woman's version of a coat, fitted to the waist and flared over the hips. They came in flowered calico for summer and wool or velvet for winter. Most older and married ladies wore a linen and lace cap at all times, with a light headscarf-like love hood over it. Hair was worn a little longer but still with the back hair taken up into a tight bun and the side hair curled and hanging loose.

DIFFERENT GROUPS

Between 1690 and 1770, many new religious groups arrived in America. During the 1680s and 1690s Jewish immigrants arrived, settling in the developing urban centers of New York, Savannah, and Charleston. Anabaptists and French Huguenots also began to arrive in large numbers. German immigrants of all denominations—Lutherans, German Reformed, Mennonites, Moravians, Baptists, and Catholics—as well as British Methodists came during this period, as did English and Welsh Baptists, and Scottish and Irish Presbyterians.

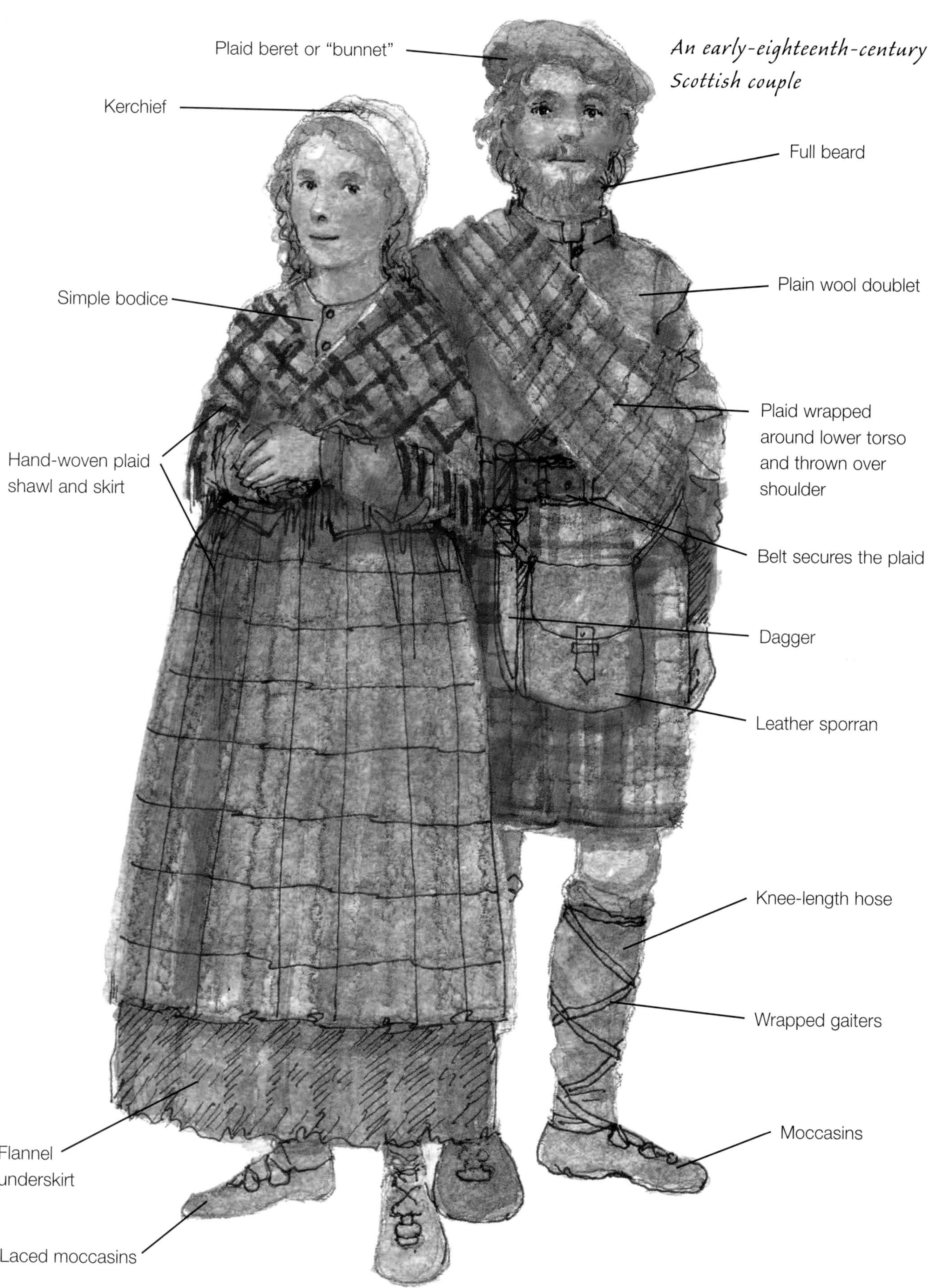

An early-eighteenth-century Scottish couple

SHOWY LADIES

"Besides these notable pockets, they likewise wore scissors and pincushions suspended from their girdles by red ribbons, or, among the more opulent and showy classes, by brass and even silver chains, indubitable tokens of thrifty housewives and industrious spinsters. I cannot say much in vindication of the shortness of the petticoats; it doubtless was introduced for the purpose of giving the stockings a chance to be seen, which were generally of blue Worsted, with magnificent red clocks; or perhaps to display a well-turned ankle and a neat though serviceable foot, set off by a high-heeled leathern shoe, with a large and splendid silver buckle."

An observer, and writer, Washington Irving, on New York ladies

Ethnic differences were reflected in the way people dressed. In German communities in Pennsylvania, a visitor noted that women were "always in the fields, meadows, stables, etc., and do not dislike any work whatsoever" and observed that they wore working aprons over hitched-up skirts and heavy shoes. Among the English Puritan settlers in New England, wives worked mostly in the home, and so needed little protective wear other than aprons. Coarse linen clothes were put on for messy work such as cooking, feeding the hens, and tending the herb garden. Women wore fine white aprons to protect their dark garments from lint when sewing, weaving, or lace-making and to keep the work itself clean. The aprons were finished with cording or were hemmed neatly.

POORER IMMIGRANTS

The Scottish and Irish immigrants were often quite poor and had to work as agricultural wage laborers. Merchants and craftsmen also employed them to make clothing fabrics on looms set up in their homes. Many of the poorer immigrants had been textile workers in their countries of origin—Ireland, say, or Germany. Richer merchants bought wool and flax from farmers and hired the new arrivals to work at home, spinning these materials into yarn and weaving cloth.

Below: A woman dressed as a Pilgrim plants seeds in a garden in a village near Plymouth, Massachusetts, reconstructed to commemorate America's settlers. She wears clothes of a coarse, durable fabric, in colors that will not show the dirt.

Although there were no checks or plaids in conventional seventeenth-century costume, such homemade patterned cloth was worn by both the Scots and the Irish, made into plaids, kilts and shawls. There is reason to believe that these Scottish and Irish weavers introduced their plaid-weaving skills to America. Plaids first appeared as homely rugs and blankets, but after the American Revolutionary War, they resurfaced in a different form, as the frontiersmen's and cowboys' checked shirts.

QUAKERS

Quakers had a distinct set of moral ethics. They believed that all people were equal in God's eyes, regardless of race, gender, or social status. To underline this belief, they wore plain clothes and refused to remove their hats to wealthier or more powerful individuals. Their clothes followed the classic image of Puritan costume, except that many Quakers were of the merchant and professional classes and therefore had more money to spend. Although their clothes were simple, they were of the best quality, made from beautiful silks in colors that displayed restrained taste, such as silver gray and soft cinnamon. The women allowed themselves the occasional red flannel petticoat too.

Above: Quakers attend a prayer meeting. By springing up to speak, the man in the center has caused his hat to fly off his head!
Below: Quaker wedding dresses were simple and undecorated.

CLOSE-KNIT COMMUNITIES

Outside the towns, apart from in the huge plantations of the South, the majority of people in the colonies lived on small family-run farms. The communities were close knit and often made up of groups of immigrants who had come to America already knowing one another as members of the same congregation. As rural folk, they didn't like change and stuck firmly to their traditional beliefs, way of life, and style of dress. For people who accepted the rules of their social group without question, such a life fostered a deep sense of belonging and contentment.

The groups of colonists were almost entirely self-sufficient and disapproved of any bought cloth or clothing. They grew flax to spin and weave into linen and reared sheep to be shorn for wool, and cattle for hides to be tanned for boots and shoes. A plentiful supply of wild deer

Right: More people at Plymouth: the man is wearing a buckskin jerkin; the woman is in a serviceable red gown.

SOUTHERN DRESS

"Many Negroes in Charles-Town . . . openly buy and sell sundry sorts of Wares. . . . It is apparent, that Negro Women in particular do not restrain themselves in their clothing as the law requires but dress in apparel quite gay and beyond their condition."

From the *South Carolina Gazette,* November 5, 1744

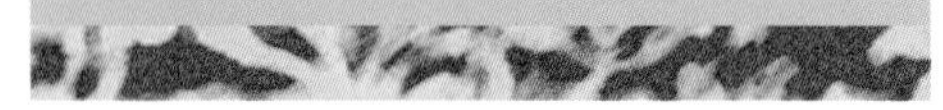

provided buckskin for clothing. Even dyeing was done at home using indigo and other native plants. This philosophy of self-help within a caring community and working in tune with the environment is a gift to the re-enactor or the producer of plays and pageants. Because people's clothes were homemade in simple shapes with no applied decoration, they are easy to re-create.

SLAVE COSTUME

In 1619, the first Africans arrived in the English American colonies, although clear evidence of the use of African Americans as slaves does not appear until 1640. Some African Americans worked as laborers in urban centers. Many of them were free, but others were still slaves. Freed slaves wore the clothes of the period as they worked alongside white laborers. In 1750, they comprised more than 10 percent of the populations of Philadelphia and New York.

There were thousands of slaves working on the huge Southern plantations, and they had no opportunity to dress with any individuality. The slaveholders were in charge of providing the clothing for this huge labor force. They ordered hundreds of yards of cheap, coarse linens (especially the German osnaburg) and woolens, hundreds of buttons, and various inexpensive ready-made items. A planter, Robert Beverly, ordered 60 "waistcoats of the cheapest color." Each male slave received a winter and a summer jacket, pants or breeches, and two shirts, while a female slave was given a jacket, a winter and a summer petticoat, and two shifts.

Slave women wore simple shift dresses in unbleached cotton or coarse, undyed linen, sometimes with a shawl around the shoulders and a striped turban on the head. The dresses were square cut and calf length and had a cord to gather the neck. Men wore shirts, simple unhemmed breeches, and vests, all in the same fabric, and straw hats. The fact that all slave clothing came from the same source ensured a uniformity of clothing. Despite this, many slaves found ways to individualize their clothing by purchasing extra garments, wearing distinctive head wraps, and accessorizing with jewelry, especially earrings. One slave painted his seams blue and drew a snake-like shape on the front of his jacket.

Slaves who worked as indoor servants fared better. Slaves working in the households or those who were favorite personal servants often received their masters' hand-me-downs. Women dressed in a maid's cotton dress and cap, and the men wore either livery or the common clothes of the working man of the period.

Above: In this painting, escaping women slaves wear simple linen shift dresses tied with colored shawls. The men and boys are in plain shirts and loose pants.

LIVERIES

Male servants wore three-piece livery uniforms whose dual color scheme was based on their master's coat of arms. The coat was often of one color, while the breeches and waistcoat were of a contrasting color. Liveries were heavily embroidered in gold or silver trim, and the buttons often had coat-of-arms-related motifs. George Washington's servants wore scarlet and off-white livery, based on his coat of arms. Thomas Jefferson's servants wore blue and scarlet liveries, trimmed in silver.

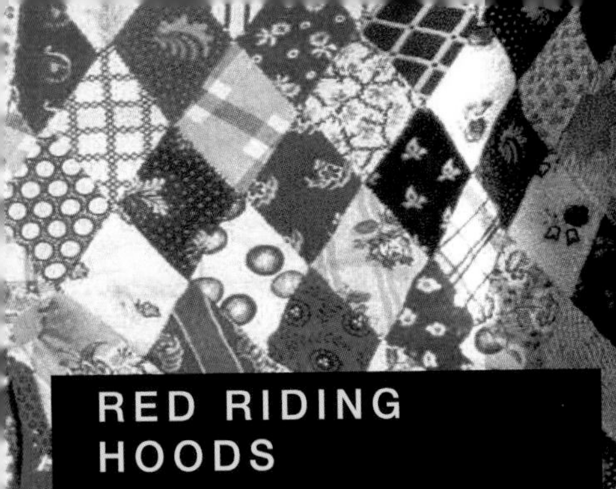

RED RIDING HOODS

In cold weather, the most popular female outer garment was the hooded wool cloak, and the most popular color for this was red. A visitor mentioned that almost every Virginia lady in the eighteenth century owned a red cloak.

CHAPTER 4

Made in America

DEMAND OUTSTRIPS SUPPLY

In the 1660s, the British government placed limitations on importation, demanding that all goods bound for the colonies be shipped through England or Wales first. This meant that there was no direct trade with other European countries except by smuggling. In 1700, the population of the English colonies was 250,000 (with 30,000 slaves). By 1750, it had grown to 1.25 million (with slaves comprising 20 percent of that number). A crisis loomed, since eighteenth-century colonial America was unable to satisfy the demands of its growing population. Despite a certain amount of home production, most textiles in the first half of the eighteenth century were imported from Britain. As the American colonies began their march toward independence from Britain, the movement toward "homespun production" was born. However, the demand for foreign-imported goods, especially woolens, linens, cottons, and, to a lesser extent, silks, was large, since home production was insufficient.

Above: This early-eighteenth-century painting by Watteau, of a courtly scene in an idyllic country setting, sums up the romantic, exotic mood of the time.

During this era trade opened up with the Far East through the British East India Company. The most popular imports were Indian cottons and Chinese silks. Favorite among Indian cottons were printed chintzes, with their strong colors and polished surface. The popularity of these items was so strong on both sides of the Atlantic that a law was passed in Britain to allow the passage of those goods through British ports, but only for re-export purposes. This meant that the colonial Americans, unlike the British, could own garments made of these exotic fabrics.

The wealthiest Americans still looked to the English aristocracy for guidance. The highest position in the colonies belonged to the royal governor, invariably a member of the English aristocracy. The governors and their circles were informed about the latest British fashions through letters, visitors, and their own sons, who were often sent back to England to study. An Englishman visiting Boston in 1740 wrote: "Both the ladies and the gentlemen dress and appear as gay in common as courtiers in England in coronation or birthday."

POCKETS

Women's gowns didn't have sewn-in pockets. Instead women carried their accessories in small bags, called pockets. These were fastened around the waist with linen or cotton ties, and worn under the skirts and petticoats. Pockets were usually made of linen or cotton fabric. They were sometimes heavily embroidered with silk thread or embellished with needlework. A popular gift item, pockets were often named in wills.

WOMEN'S COSTUME

Throughout the eighteenth century, the silhouette of a woman's gown was cone-shaped, with a tightly fitted bodice and full skirt. The bodice was worn over a shift and a tightly laced corset. The skirt, its fullness held out by hoops, was worn over a petticoat. Very often the skirt was open at the front to reveal the petticoat, in which case the look and the color of the petticoat became an important part of the overall design. Sometimes the color of the petticoat would blend in with the gown, but more often than not it would be in strong contrast to it.

It was common for the bodice to be slit open to allow for the removable decorative triangular piece, or stomacher, to be pinned or laced in the

Right: This 1748 portrait of a wealthy woman is by the American colonial era painter, Robert Feke. The woman's gown, with its low, lace-trimmed neckline, is made in the best-quality heavy silk taffeta in a beautiful shade of pink. The fabric would have been extremely expensive.

BRIDAL WEAR

In most cases, brides were expected to wear their bridal gowns long after their wedding day. Therefore, they chose a dress that would be suitable for many future occasions, either of patterned silk or a sensible color, such as dark brown. Only wealthy brides were able to have a one-of-a-kind dress. These were white or white combined with silver. Fans were often specially designed for weddings and given as commemorative wedding gifts.

middle. Sometimes stomachers were plain, but often they were heavily embroidered and decorated. Since stomachers were detachable, they could be worn with different gowns and allowed the wearer to explore her talents of "mix and match." The backs of the gowns mostly followed two distinct styles. The pleats either fell loosely from the shoulders (called "sack" or "robe à la Française") or they were stitched down close to the back ("robe à l'Anglaise").

The bodice neckline was rectangular and decorated with a cotton or lace ruffle. The sleeves were narrow and finished below the elbow in cascading ruffles, which often matched the ruffles around the neckline. Many of the gowns worn by ordinary middle-class American women didn't have stomachers but were fully closed at the center front, usually with hooks and eyes. The edges of the front skirt opening were often finished with pinking. The neck opening was covered by a neckerchief, usually a triangular piece of cotton, either for warmth or modesty. Mitts and gloves often accompanied the neckerchiefs.

Right: A well-to-do couple in period clothes take part in a historical re-enactment at Colonial Williamsburg.

Left: In this portrait by Robert Feke, Massachusetts gentleman Isaac Winslow is shown wearing a long, ivory-colored satin waistcoat, richly embroidered with gold thread. This luxurious garment is in stark contrast to the dark brown velvet of his topcoat.

MEN'S COSTUME

At the beginning of the eighteenth century, men's suits consisted of three major pieces: coat, waistcoat, and breeches. The full-skirted coat reached down to the knee or more often below it. The sleeves were full, with broad cuffs. Often, the skirts of men's coats were stiffened with wire to help them stand out. There was no collar. The waistcoat, worn under the coat, came to above the knee. The breeches were knee-length, with buttons at the center front and gathers at the back to facilitate movement. The fabric and color of waistcoats were often in contrast to the fabric and color of the coat and breeches.

In a letter to his English tailor in 1733, Jonathan Belcher, the governor of Massachusetts (1682–1757), ordered two suits: one of yellow grogram (silk and mohair) and one of "very good silk." "It must be a substantial silk, because you'll see I have ordered it to be trimm'd rich . . . I say, let it be a handsome compleat suit, and two pair of breeches to each suit."

JEWELRY

Very little jewelry was worn in this time. The chief decorations on men's costume were buttons; some women had lockets and bracelets. The most common jewelry items were rings, especially mourning rings, which were given to all the mourners at the funeral. Most well-to-do men accumulated a large number of mourning rings. Another popular funeral gift was gloves: at society funerals, over a thousand pairs of gloves could be given away.

WASHABLE DRAWERS

Many men wore washable linen or cotton drawers under their breeches, especially in colder weather. George Washington ordered breeches from London, with clear instructions that they were to be worn over drawers.

SHOES

Women's shoes were made of brocaded silk and satin and of leather. Men's shoes and boots were for the most part made of leather. Women's shoes had straps over the instep, which were fastened by removable buckles. For the upper classes, these buckles were decorative and made of finer materials, such as silver or brass, inlaid with jewels. Buckles for the lower classes were made of cheap metal. Shoes were often ordered by foot length since there were no commercial sizes. Also, shoes were made on a straight last, which meant there was no distinction between the left and right foot.

Wealthy men such as Belcher would likely have owned about fifty fine cotton or linen shirts, the garment worn closest to the skin. He would also have owned a number of neck stocks, the precursor of modern neckties. Typically, a neck stock was a width of fabric (fine cotton or linen), pleated or gathered and attached to narrow tabs. Another form of neck decoration was a decorative lace ruffle attached to the neck opening, which was usually balanced by lace ruffles around the shirtsleeves. Most men continued to wear white, tightly curled shoulder-length wigs.

GENTLEMEN OF LEISURE

Less formal clothing, usually worn at home, was called "undress." Among the most popular clothing items of undress for gentlemen of leisure was a loose gown, called a banyan. Banyans were worn with caps and turbans

Right: At a shop in Colonial Williamsburg, re-enactors make leather shoes for the town's citizens.

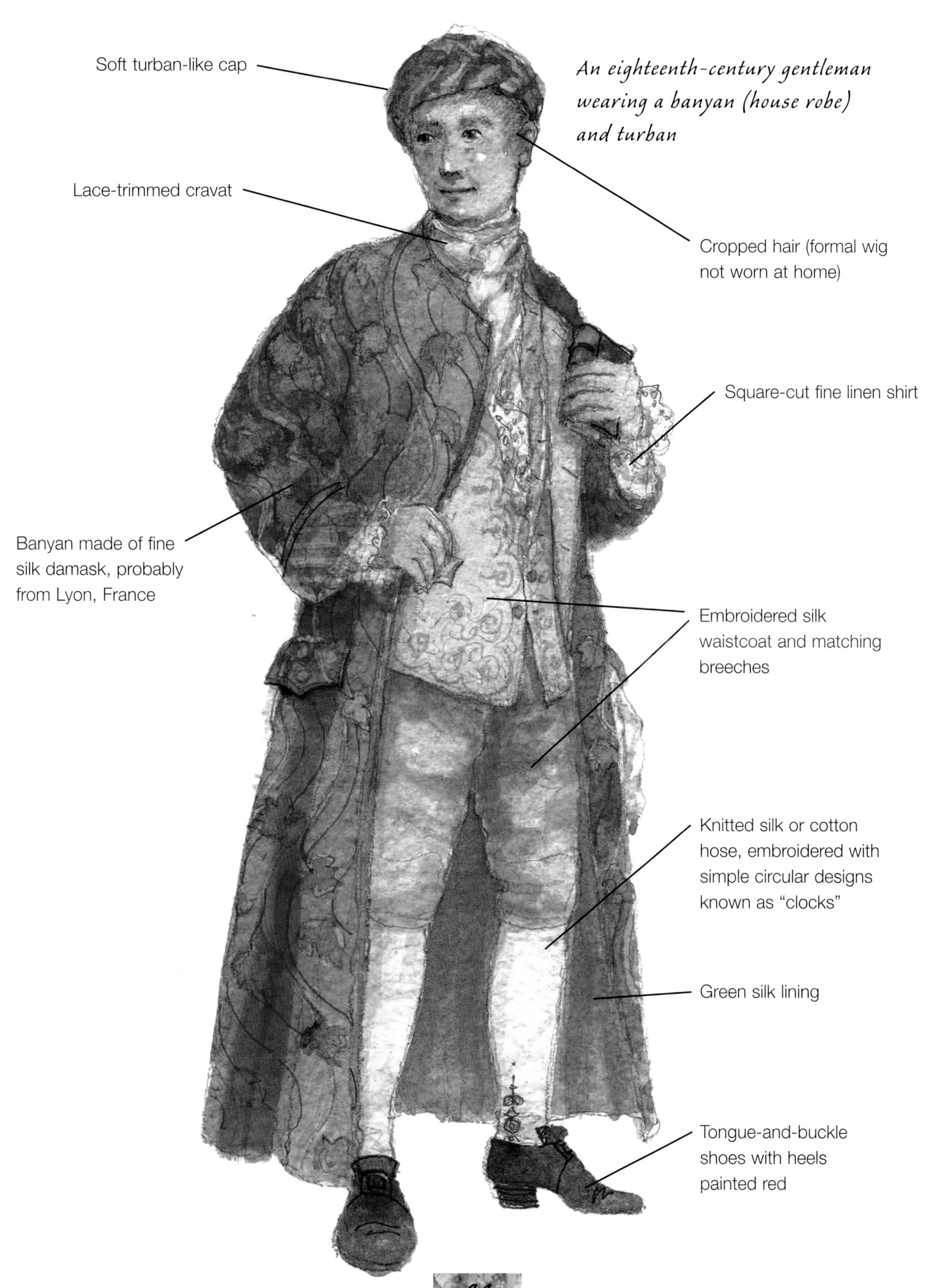

An eighteenth-century gentleman wearing a banyan (house robe) and turban

Left: Unusually for a banyan, this one is cut with a fitted back, but the most interesting thing about it is that it is made of a beautiful diamond patchwork.

(men took off their wigs), over shirts, breeches, and stockings, and sometimes with waistcoats and cravats. Engraver and silversmith Nathaniel Hurd was painted by artist John Singleton Copley wearing his taupe silk banyan, richly lined with salmon silk, over a black waistcoat with gold metal buttons and an open-collared white shirt, paired with a simple black silk cap.

Usually banyans were made of silks, linens, cottons, or even wools for winter use. In the *Boston Weekley Gazette*, in 1738, a shopkeeper advertised banyans made of "worsted, damask and brocaded stuffs; also Scotch plaids and callimancos." Even very staid and conservative gentlemen were adventurous when it came to their banyans. Dr. Edward Holyoke owned one of bright orange, with pink and brown stripes. Banyans were especially popular in the Southern states, where the lightweight cotton or linen loose gowns could be a welcome alternative to coats in the hot summer months. Very often, Virginian gentlemen had their coats made of unlined cotton or linen so that they were not too heavy and hot to wear.

WORKING-CLASS COSTUME

The majority of the colonists, however, spent their lives in hard physical labor. Working-class clothing was made of sturdier materials: coarse woolens, linens, and cottons that could endure wear and tear. Cheap, British printed cottons, imitative of Indian chintzes, were extremely popular.

Full-skirted gowns were impractical for work, so women often hiked the skirts up or wore shorter dresses, called "bed gowns." For bed gowns, the skirt and bodice were cut in one piece that opened at the front, and was very often held in place with pins or aprons. The sleeves of the bed gown could be rolled up for work. Although the showing of one's elbows was considered unseemly, working women would certainly have needed to do this to get a job done!

Above: In this re-enactment scene, a working man wears rough fabric breeches.

Another popular working-class woman's garment was a fitted jacket, often called a "waistcoat" or "caraco." It was either laced down the front or closed with buttons and worn over the petticoats. Aprons, made of checked linen or cotton, were worn for everyday use, while aprons of white linen or cotton were reserved for special occasions.

Working-class men often wore shorter jackets, with or without sleeves. The sleeved jackets had more room in them to allow movement. The sleeveless jackets could be worn over shirts, especially in the South. Knitted sleeves could be added to these jackets for warmth. Instead of stockings, farmers wore fabric leggings, often made of leather. In the hot summer months, farmers wore long smocks made of linen or cotton over leggings or breeches, with straw hats as protection against the sun. They often tied neckerchiefs around their necks. Very popular working-class garments were leather breeches, sometimes dubbed "the blue jeans of the eighteenth century" because of their durability and comfort.

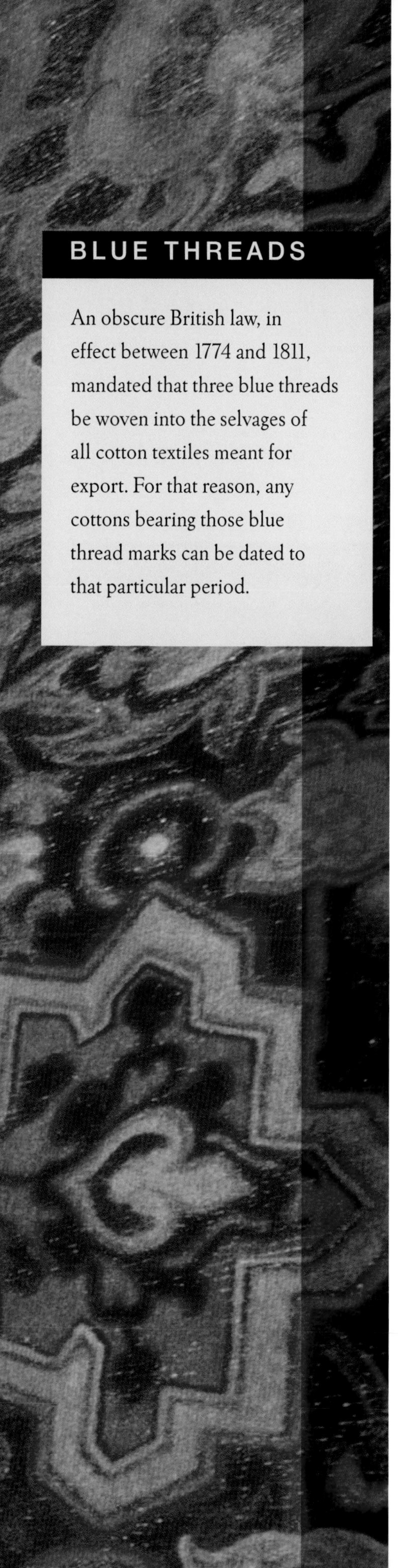

BLUE THREADS

An obscure British law, in effect between 1774 and 1811, mandated that three blue threads be woven into the selvages of all cotton textiles meant for export. For that reason, any cottons bearing those blue thread marks can be dated to that particular period.

CHAPTER 5

Military Uniforms

By 1750, Britain and France both wanted to secure their claims in North America, especially in the vast territory known as the Ohio Country, stretching between the Appalachian Mountains and the Mississippi River and from the Great Lakes to the Gulf of Mexico. This conflict of interest resulted in the French and Indian War (1754–63), named after the two main opponents of the British: the royal French army and numerous Native American tribes who fought on the French side (even though some tribes, such as the Iroquois Confederacy, were allied with the British).

The war officially ended with the Treaty of Paris in 1763 and resulted in the British conquest of all French territories east of the Mississippi River and of Spanish Florida. British rule now spanned all of eastern North America, from Hudson Bay to the Mississippi. Despite a resounding victory, the war doubled the national debt. To ease this difficult economic situation, the British Crown imposed a series of tax laws on the colonies. This ultimately contributed to the beginning of the American Revolutionary War (1775–83).

Above: In the 1992 movie *The Last of the Mohicans*, based on the James Fenimore Cooper novel set during the French and Indian War, Hawkeye (Daniel Day-Lewis) is marched away by British redcoats.

UNIFORMS OF THE FRENCH AND INDIAN WAR

Above: Re-enactors dressed as French troops mark the 250th anniversary of the Battle of Fort Ontario, fought in 1756.

The British soldiers were universally known as "redcoats" because the majority of regiments wore the familiar coats of scarlet wool, with black leather accessories. In 1702, red had been adopted as the official color of the British Army when the Duke of Marlborough ordered that "officers be all clothed in red, plain and uniform, which is expected they should wear on all marches and other duties as well as days of Review." Red was a cheap dye, but it also signified the red cross of St. George, the patron saint of England.

The redcoat's folds were buttoned back to form lapels. The buttons were gilded and bore the regimental number and the crown of George III, ultimate commander of the British Army. The uniform also included a waistcoat, a stock, gaiters reaching just above the knee, and a cocked hat. The ordinary regiments' coat facings were yellow, while royal and household regiments had facings of blue. These foot soldiers often carried a bulk of articles weighing about 60 pounds (27 kilograms). Those articles included a belt over the left shoulder that supported a cartouche (cartridge) box, a belt around the waist supporting a bayonet and a short sword, and a knapsack containing extra clothing, a blanket, and a haversack with provisions. Artillery units wore blue coats and white breeches; musicians' uniforms were white, while drummers and fifers wore yellow.

The famous General James Wolfe, whose defeat of the French forces at the Battle of Quebec in 1759 was instrumental in bringing about the British victory, was said to have encouraged a simpler version of the uniform. It consisted of a red jacket with sleeves, over which a sleeveless red coat could be worn for parade or for active service.

The officers' uniforms were similar to those of the men, even though the officers were usually given some latitude. They also wore a small steel plate, called a gorget, around their necks. Like the buttons, the gorget was usually gilded and bore the regimental insignia. (Originally, it was a large steel part of medieval armor that protected the throat.)

The French soldiers' uniform consisted of grayish white coats and breeches, with collars, cuffs, and waistcoats made of either red or blue wool, depending on the regiment. Buttons were either pewter or brass, and their tricornes (three-pointed hats) were trimmed with silver or gold lace. The Royal Artillery regiment had blue coats with red breeches and red waistcoats.

Above: From the eighteenth century onward, the gorget became primarily ornamental, serving only as a symbolic accessory on officers' uniforms.

POWDERED HAIR

The British officers' hair was powdered and cued (put into a tail), and their faces were clean-shaven. Soldiers of each company were issued pounds of flour for the hair powdering; each soldier was allowed half a pound per week. Soldiers with short hair had false cues of leather with the tuft of hair attached at the end.

MILITIA GROUPS

Most American colonies formed and financed their own voluntary militia units, assembled periodically to protect their territories, especially against the attacks of the various Native American tribes. These units fought against the French alongside the British Army. The militia had no fixed uniforms, and each regiment came up with its own design. The North Carolina regiments wore blue coats with red lapels and breeches; the Pennsylvania regiment had uniforms of green and scarlet. In Georgia, a militia group from the city of Darien, founded by early Scottish settlers, was dressed in Highland fashion. Very often, the local officers followed English customs, as was the case in Virginia and Maryland. George Washington was the colonel of the Virginia militia, and he gained valuable experience fighting with the British.

RANGERS

Rangers were men who patrolled the outskirts of the settlements to gather intelligence on the enemy and help mount quick raids. Early rangers used their own clothing and weapons and often wore Native American moccasins. During the French and Indian War, numerous ranger companies were financed by the British Crown, even though they weren't officially recognized as a part of the British Army. Some were described

Above: Spencer Tracy (right) wears a version of the Rogers' Rangers' uniform in the 1940 movie *Northwest Passage*. The rangers borrowed much of their clothing from the Native Americans, especially the use of fringed buckskin and soft moccasins.

as wearing civilian wide-brimmed hats and olive-cloth coats, buckskin breeches, leather Native American leggings, and black leather shoes. In 1758, Major George Scott mentions a hooded cloak, a leather cap, "a coat just the same as the common coat of regular soldiers, only the skirts are shorter, so as not to fatigue the men on the long march."

Other rangers, in 1761, were described as wearing short red coats with a brown collar and lining, a brown waistcoat, linen drawers, and leather jockey caps with an oak leaf or branch painted on the left side. The famous Rogers' Rangers wore a short green coat with a green collar and cuffs, a green waistcoat, buckskin breeches, and a green, Scottish-style bonnet.

Writing in 1799, Captain James Smith remembered the strange uniform of his rangers: "As we enlisted our men, we dressed them uniformly in the Indian manner, with breech-clouts, leggings, mockesons and green shrouds, which we wore in the same manner as the Indians do, and nearly as the Highlanders wore their plaids. In place of hats, we wore red handkerchiefs and painted our faces red and black, like Indian warriors." Some Native American warriors also served as rangers, and they wore a mixture of native and European dress.

Above: In the 1985 movie *Revolution*, Dexter Fletcher and Al Pacino wear the suitably bedraggled clothing of the colonial rebels.

DYEING SHIRTS

"They take a piece of tow cloth [linen] that is stout, and put it in a tan vat until it has the shade of the fallen dry leaf. Then they made a kind of frock of it, reaching down below the knee, open before, with a large cape. They wrap it around them tight on a march, and tie it with their belt, on which hangs their tomahawk."

In 1775, an observer describes the Philadelphia riflemen's shirts

UNIFORMS OF THE AMERICAN REVOLUTION

The early Revolutionary soldiers were citizens carrying arms, not yet a professional army with designated uniforms. Many soldiers wore their own clothing or continued to wear the uniforms of their militia units. Rebel forces were often noted for their haphazard attire and haggard appearance, with worn-out shoes and stockings. A boycott of British goods combined with British naval blockades meant there was no access to materials needed to supply the Revolutionary forces with new uniforms. Most Americans supported the troops and helped out by providing homespun clothing.

HUNTING SHIRTS

In 1775, George Washington was appointed commander in chief of the American Continental Army. One of his major concerns was to find adequate clothing for his troops, especially in freezing winter conditions.

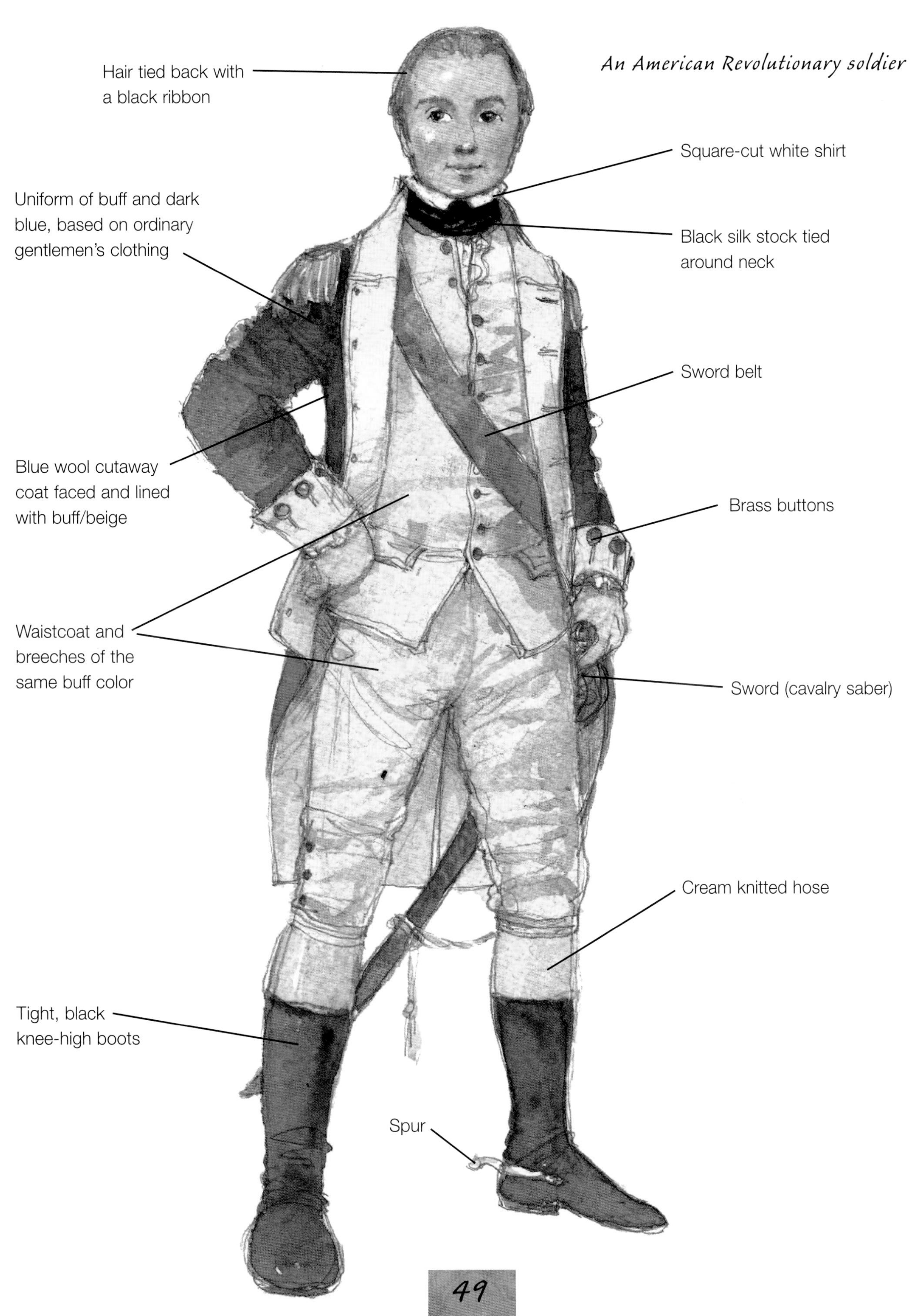
An American Revolutionary soldier
Hair tied back with a black ribbon
Square-cut white shirt
Uniform of buff and dark blue, based on ordinary gentlemen's clothing
Black silk stock tied around neck
Sword belt
Blue wool cutaway coat faced and lined with buff/beige
Brass buttons
Waistcoat and breeches of the same buff color
Sword (cavalry saber)
Cream knitted hose
Tight, black knee-high boots
Spur

A PAMPERED LIFE

"You have no idea of the life of continued amusement I live in . . . and most elegantly dressed am I for a ball this evening. . . . The dress is more ridiculous and pretty than anything I ever saw—a great quantity of different colored feathers on the head beside a thousand other things. . . . The hair dressed very high."

Rebecca Franks, a visitor to New York in 1778. Despite the war, many members of the upper class still enjoyed balls and an active social life.

Instead of heavy, three-piece regimental coats, which could weigh between 10 and 15 pounds (4.5 and 6.8 kilograms), Washington advocated lightweight hunting shirts made of linen. These shirts had a full front opening and functioned as a coat because they could be worn over many layers in cold weather. Washington appealed to various governors to procure linen to make hunting or Native American shirts for his troops. He said these shirts were cheaper and more convenient.

Washington was especially concerned about protecting his soldiers' legs and recommended the use of Native American stockings, or leggings. These were described in 1784 by J. F. D. Smythe, an explorer, as "made of coarse woolen cloth, that either wrapped around loosely and tied with garters, or laced upon the outside. . . . These are great defense and preservative." The costume of the Native American was an amalgamation of the original attire (which often included animal skins) and European textiles and other trade goods. Kentucky Native Americans were described by observer John Filson in 1784 as wearing "shirt of the English make, on which they bestow innumerable broaches to adorn it, a sort of cloth boots and mockasons, which are shoes of a make peculiar

Right: In this portrait by Charles Wilson Peale, George Washington is depicted wearing a dark jacket with red facings, a red waistcoat and breeches, and a gorget.

Above: A group of men in American Revolutionary War military uniforms re-enact a bayonet charge during a celebration of George Washington's birthday in Alexandria, Virginia.

to the Indians, ornamented with porcupine quills." African Americans fought on both sides in the Revolutionary War. The British were the first to recruit from the black population, offering freedom (and a uniform) in return for joining up. Washington eventually accepted African Americans, who made up at least two regiments and who were also set free in this way.

AMERICAN INDEPENDENCE

The French soldiers, under the Count of Rochambeau, arrived in America in 1781, this time as allies of the Continental Army. They wore coats of white broadcloth, trimmed in green, with white shirts and pants, and bicornes (these two-cornered hats were later made famous by Napoleon Bonaparte). British general Charles Cornwallis surrendered to Washington in 1781 at Yorktown, after his army suffered a huge defeat from the combined French and American forces. This signaled the end of war. The peace was officially signed in 1783 in the Treaty of Paris, where Britain ceded to America all its lands east of Mississippi and south of the Great Lakes.

After the victory at Yorktown, blue became the official color of the new independent American army. The intricacies of the uniforms of the French and Indian War and the American Revolutionary War can be found on many re-enactment Web sites.

CHAPTER 6

Textiles

OLD NAMES

There are some wonderful names for the colors of colonial costume dyes: they include philomot (feuille-mort, or dead leaf color), murry (the dark wine color of mulberry fruits), treen (the color of burr maple, a rich brown), gridolin (gris-de-lin, or gray), flax (blue), puce (a sort of eggplant purple), stammel (red), and zaffre (sapphire) blue.

DYES AND COLOR

In colonial times, the dyeing of clothes was a complicated process. It was difficult to achieve pretty colors, and this made the finished result rare, expensive, and highly valued. Chemical dyes had not yet been invented. Instead, dyes were derived from roots, fruits and vegetables (such as

Below: A Pilgrim interpreter sews clothes made of brightly dyed fabrics outside her home at the living history museum near Plymouth.

mulberry, oak gall, or onion skins), or animals (the costly squid ink and cochineal from beetles). A mordant (fixative) was used to make the color more permanent. Common salt, vinegar, or alum, boiled with the main ingredients, caused the dye to penetrate the fibers better. Different mordants produced variations of color. It was a skilled craft—no wonder anyone who could afford it wore cheerful colors!

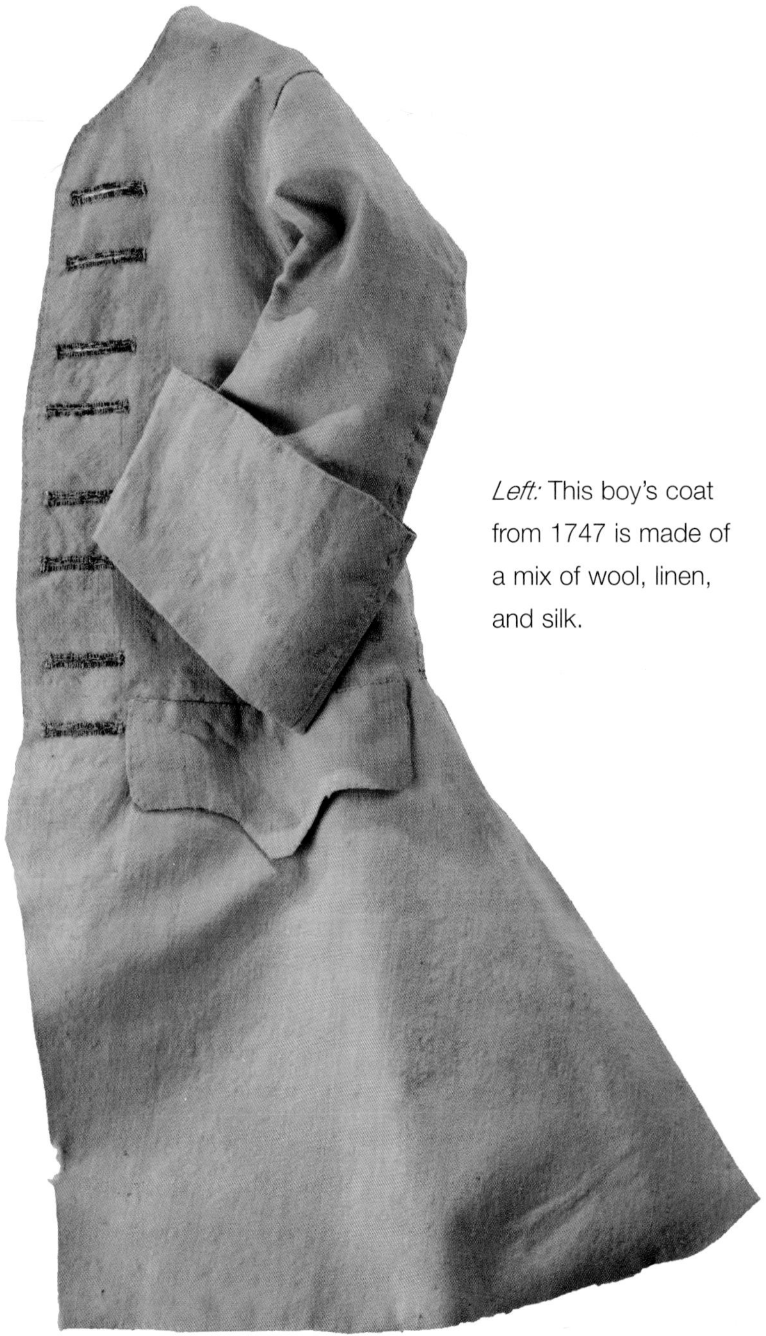

Left: This boy's coat from 1747 is made of a mix of wool, linen, and silk.

WOOL PRODUCTION

The main fibers for textiles were wool and linen. The simplest and most ancient of textiles, wool from sheep, either woven or felted, has been used to clothe people for thousands of years. In seventeenth-century England, the wool trade was incredibly important to the national economy, and many thousands of people were involved in wool production. It is believed that the production of a length of cloth gave work to thirty craftspeople.

The textile industry fought hard against any threat to the wool trade from foreign production. Wool producers from the colonies were forbidden to make their own cloth. Instead, they were instructed to send the raw wool to England, where it could be made into fabric, which was then sent back out to America to be cut and sewn into garments. However, many colonists bypassed these regulations, and resistance to this British interference grew.

STYLE TIP

Don't be tempted to put any form of shoulder padding in a man's eighteenth-century coat. The modern male silhouette of wide shoulders and slim hips wasn't fashionable then.

SPINNING AND WEAVING

Spinning is the drawing and twisting of fibrous materials into a continuous length. The fibers are drawn out to the required thickness, and a spinning implement (twist) is used to bind the fibers together. The task of the spinster is to draw out the fibers and guide the twist. In colonial times, the cleaned and carded wool was usually spun by the women of the house, then set up onto a loom and woven, using a shuttle, into cloth of varying weights. The wool could be dyed before weaving or

HAND LOOMS

A hand loom consisted of four wood uprights joined at the top and bottom to form a box-like framework. There were wood rollers between both pairs of uprights, one for the weft and one to collect the cloth. The weaving operation consisted of sending the shuttle containing the weft back and forth through the threads of the warp. A device operated by a treadle lifted and lowered alternate threads. A lathe hanging from the top of the loom enabled the weaver to push each thread of weft up against the cloth already woven. Before weaving could begin, the warp had to be wound onto its roller, or beam, and the threads passed through the lathe and fastened to the cloth beam. The warp threads had to be dressed with a flour-and-water paste to make them strong enough to withstand the weaving process.

as finished fabric. As in England and Europe, weaving was a natural adjunct to small-scale farming, and all the family were involved—the children carding, the wife spinning, and the husband weaving.

The cloth was often "fulled" to make it stronger and more weatherproof. It was not a process normally undertaken at home, since it required water power to drive great wooden hammers that beat the cloth until the fibers interlocked, much like felt-making. The finish is much like felt, which is why costumers sometimes use felt to replicate fulled cloth. But the fulling of woven material produces a far stronger product than simple felting. Boiling your wool fabric will produce a similar result.

LINEN

In 1619, the Virginia Company instructed the colony in Jamestown to promote flax-harvesting. The stockholders hoped that the colonists would use this ancient crop to realize a profit and diversify their labors.

Right: An eighteenth-century English painting of a lady's maid soaping linen indicates the widespread use of this durable fabric. The servant girl is surprisingly well dressed, in a painted silk gown.

Left: A piece of English linen, embroidered with silks, from the early 1600s.

The enterprises didn't make much money, but they show that flax for linen-making was being cultivated from an early date. English law decreed that any area of planting must contain about 5 percent of linen to produce enough cloth for private use and for sale.

Linen-making was a labor-intensive, smelly business, but the results are beautiful and durable. Linen was made into shirts, chemises, sheets, and towels and knitted into stockings and mittens. The rougher linen was used to make sails and even rope.

COTTON

Cotton was imported from India via the cotton mills of England and the textile printers of Holland in the eighteenth century. The newly fashionable and very beautiful chintz patterns were not shipped directly from India itself but through British ports. Cotton was grown in the

STYLE TIP

The weight and drape of fustian is ideal for American colonial costume-making, especially for working people. It can be made into jackets, vests, breeches, and women's bodices, jackets, and overskirts. Sometimes called "linen union," it's available from furnishing fabric stores. Otherwise, heavy furnishing linen, thoroughly washed through a hot washing machine cycle to soften and shrink it, is another possibility.

PRINTED FABRICS

Floral prints were the most popular for ladies' gowns. According to the *Pennsylvania Gazette* in 1750, the house of Benjamin Franklin was broken into and "the following things feloniously taken away, a double necklace of gold beads, a woman's long scarlet cloak almost new, with a double cape, a woman's gown, of brocaded printed cotton, very remarkable, the ground dark, with large red roses, and other large and yellow flowers, with blue in some flowers, with many green leaves."

STYLE TIP

If you are re-creating a wealthy person's formal costume, there really is no substitute for silk—polyester fabric won't do. Fortunately, reasonably priced silks intended for upscale cushions and curtains can be found in fabric stores.

Southern states. From the eighteenth century, huge cotton plantations dependent on slave labor made their owners very rich. American cotton was used to produce homespun clothes during the colonial period, although fashionable people preferred imported cottons for their summer dresses and pinafores since it was of a finer quality and cheaper than the American fabric.

The first cotton-based cloths to be produced outside India were fustians, which were cloths with a linen warp and a cotton weft. Fustian was an excellent, durable fabric, widely used for tough, lightweight clothing. It was being produced in America from the early seventeenth century. The increasing demand for linen warp for the expanding cotton industry boosted flax production.

SILK IN THE COLONIES

For thousands of years, silk has been considered a luxury trade good par excellence because it fetches a high price, is relatively easy to transport, and is always in demand among the wealthy. It is therefore not surprising that James I and subsequent English sovereigns encouraged the production of this textile among the settlers of Virginia. Unfortunately, silkworm caterpillars are very fussy, and they didn't like the native black

Below: In this engraving from 1748, women examine silkworm eggs before placing them into boxes for hatching.

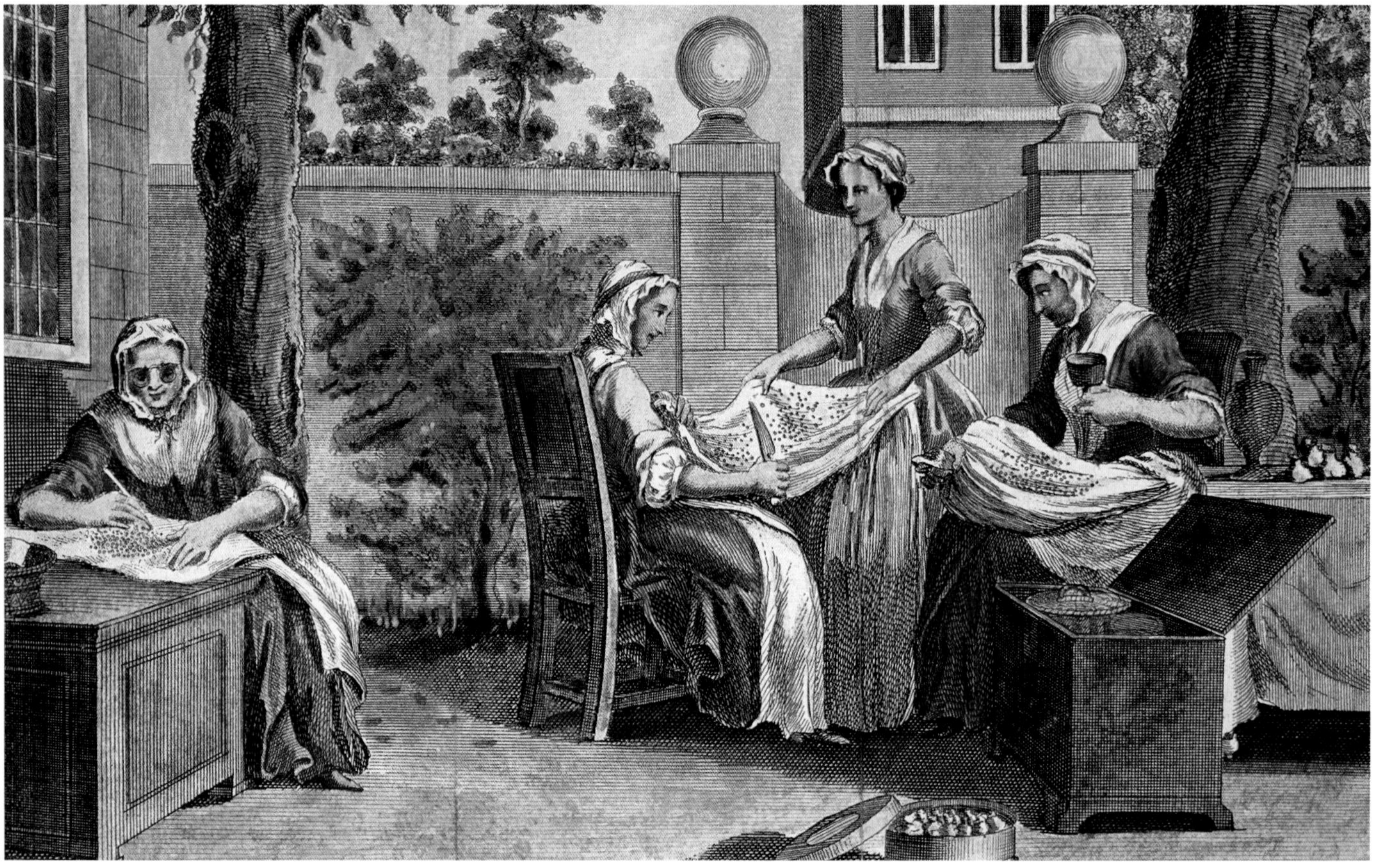

A fashionable young lady of Virginia, around 1770

FASHION BABIES

"Fashion babies" were dolls dressed in the latest fashion styles sent to America from London, even though they often originated in Paris. Another way of disseminating fashion ideas was through paper dolls, and yet another was *Godey's Lady's Book*, one of the first American fashion magazines.

STYLE TIP

Ladies going outdoors always wore a hat, both as a fashion statement and to protect against the elements. Hats had shallow, flat crowns and wide brims and were made of straw. Often, straw hats were completely covered with fabric and obscured with trim and flowers. Indoors, girls and ladies wore linen, cotton, or lace caps, often with an added ruffle. The caps were practical items since they could be washed easily and functioned as a protective layer against dust and dirt. Older women often wore mobcaps, which had a high crown, a flat border that went around the face, and two hanging side pieces (called lappets) that could be left loose or tied. Later in the eighteenth century, a calash, a collapsible bonnet of silk and cane, became popular.

Above: Margaret Kemble Gage, the American-born wife of the commander in chief of British forces in America, is pictured wearing a fine pink silk gown.

mulberries, nor did the settlers have the time or skill to cultivate the human-dependent silkworms. The success of tobacco—a much more easily cultivated cash crop—ensured the initial failure of silk production in the colonies.

In about 1760, Nathaniel Aspinwall of Mansfield, Connecticut, attempted to produce American-grown silk. He planted a mulberry orchard in town and brought the first silkworm eggs to Mansfield. Three-quarters of the people in Mansfield raised silkworms in their homes. The men planted the trees, and the women and children gathered the leaves, cared for the worms, and reeled and spun the raw silk. A spare room, an attic, a barn loft, or an outbuilding was used as a cocoonery. But this production couldn't compete with the sophistication or price of imported silks, and the silkworm farms all but died out.

Raw silk from China and Byzantium was made into fabric in France, Italy, and England. It was then exported to America, where, as in Europe, it was made into fashionable and expensive garments. It was the basis of a huge range of fabrics, from the finest shot taffetas to jaquard brocades and even silk velvet. Colored silk thread was used to embroider men's formal coats and vests and ladies' fichus and petticoats.

EMBROIDERY

For the wealthy, the eighteenth century was a period of great splendor, and the clothing reflected this. Silk fabrics were embellished by hand with ornate embroidery. Techniques included metal-thread work, silk embroidery, quilting, tambour, Hollie Point, stump work, and knotting. The larger pieces of fabric to be embroidered were fixed to a square wooden frame attached to a stand, with the piece to be worked stretched between opposite sides. Another method was to use specially made wood embroidery hoops. The fabric was laid over the smaller hoop, and the larger hoop was pressed down and tightened to keep the material taut. Both methods are still in use today, and equipment can be found at specialist craft stores or on the Internet.

Below left: A lady's embroidered jacket from around 1625.
Below: A gentleman's embroidered linen waistcoat from around 1760.

Glossary

alum The most effective mordant (literally, "something that bites") or fixative for dyestuffs. It is available at any dye or chemical supply store.

barilla Small-leaved, salt-tolerant plants that, until the nineteenth century, were the primary source of soda ash, used in soap-making.

baroque Describes something that is elaborate, with many details.

bicorne A type of eighteenth-century hat made with a circular brim folded up to produce two (bi-) points.

buff A soft, flexible, undyed thick leather, used for seventeenth-century military coats.

callimanco A wool fabric, glossy on the surface, woven with a satin twill and checkered in the warp so that the checks are seen on one side only. Callimanco was used extensively in the eighteenth century to make shoes and durable outer garments.

carded Combed and untangled wool, ready for spinning.

cartridge pleating A method of gathering large amounts of fabric to a small waistband or shoulder seam without adding bulk. Cartridge pleating also makes the fabric spring away from the waist or shoulder more than other kinds of pleating or gathering. It was popular during the sixteenth century for attaching full skirts to waistbands and bodices.

casaque A man's traveling cloak that can be turned into a coat by buttoning the side and underarm seams.

coif A close-fitting cap made of white linen and tied under the chin. Coifs were sometimes embroidered or edged with lace.

dimity A lightweight sheer cotton fabric with small raised stripes woven into the weft.

fifer A person who plays the fife, a kind of flute used in marching bands.

fixed/fixing (as with starch) The use of glue-like starch to make a fabric rigid.

flax A blue-flowered plant from which linen is made.

goffering A method of ironing complex figure-eight pleats into a ruff or cap.

Hollie Point A white-work embroidery technique, hollie, or holy, point was worked by nuns.

houppelande A garment worn by both men and women in the Middle Ages. Usually cut as a complete circle and fitted to the upper body by means of stitched pleats, the houppelande could be knee length (on men) or floor length (both sexes).

Middle Ages The era between 1000 CE and 1400 CE. Also referred to as "medieval."

oak gall A growth caused by an insect found on oak trees. The blackish liquid obtained from the gall is used in dyeing textiles and leather.

osnaburg A coarse type of plain fabric named after the city of Osnabrück in Germany.

pinked A decorative edge where the fabric is cut in a zigzag fashion.

samare A woman's jacket. In the early seventeenth century, it was closely fitted; by 1650, it was less fitted, more like a house or dressing jacket.

shuttle A cigar-shaped implement used in weaving. The weft thread is wound onto the shuttle and taken through the warp threads.

stump work Also called raised work, stump work uses padding, decoratively knotted thread, and attached pieces of embroidery.

tambour A circular embroidery frame, like a tambourine, where the work is stretched over a hoop and held in place by a second, slightly larger hoop.

treadle A lever that a loom operator presses with his or her foot to turn a wheel that makes the loom work.

tricorne A type of eighteenth-century hat made with a circular brim folded up to produce three (tri-) points.

tucker A cloth "tucked" or folded and pinned in place to protect the garments. As in "bib and tucker"—a child's bib and apron set.

warp The long threads on a weaving loom.

weft The crosswise threads that are woven into the warp to form cloth.

yeoman A freeholder who cultivated his own land.

Further Information

BOOKS

Ashelford, Jane. *The Art of Dress. Clothes and Society, 1500–1914.* National Trust, 1999.

Barghini, Sandra. *Aspects of America: The American Museum in Britain.* Scala Publishers, 2007.

Baumgarten, Linda. *Eighteenth-Century Clothing at Williamsburg.* (*Williamsburg Decorative Arts* series). Colonial Williamsburg Foundation, 1986.

Baumgarten, Linda. *What Clothes Reveal: The Language of Clothing in Colonial and Federal America.* Yale University Press, 2002.

Chartrand, Rene, and Dave Rickman. *Colonial American Troops 1610–1774.* (*Men-at-Arms* series). Osprey Publishing, 2003.

Earle, Alice Morse. *Two Centuries of Costume in America, Volume I, (1620–1820).* First published Macmillan Company New York, 1903, reprinted Corner House, 1979.

Grierson, Su. *Dyeing and Dyestuffs.* Shire Album, 1992.

Johnson, Michael and Richard Hook. *American Woodland Indians.* (*Men-at-Arms* series). Osprey Publishing, 1990.

Leadbeater, Eliza. *Spinning and Spinning Wheels.* Shire Library, 2009.

May, Robin. *Wolfe's Army.* (*Men-at-Arms* series). Osprey Publishing, 1998.

May, Robin, and G. A. Embleton. *The British Army in North America, 1775–1783.* (*Men-at-Arms* series). Osprey Publishing, 1998.

Miller, Marla R. *The Needle's Eye: Women and Work in the Age of Revolution.* University of Massachusetts Press, 2006.

Rutt, Richard. *A History of Hand Knitting.* Interweave Press, 2003.

Smith, Bradley. *The USA—A History in Art.* Crowell, 1975.

Waugh, Norah. *The Cut of Men's Clothes: 1600–1900.* Theatre Arts Books, 1987.

WEB SITES ON COLONIAL AMERICA

Many of these Web sites have links to other, related sites.

americanhistory.about.com/od/colonialamerica/tp/earlycolonial.htm
Book and movie recommendations.

www.anniescostumes.com/early.htm
Web site with details of various early American costumes. Dress up as characters from the period, including Martha Washington, a Pilgrim or an American soldier.

www.earlyamerica.com
A history site with primary source material from eighteenth-century America. Includes short movies of noteworthy events and early American heroes, such as Benjamin Franklin and George Washington.

falcon.jmu.edu/ffamseyil/colonial.htm
A history Web site, with maps, lesson plans, bibliographies and curriculum content materials.

www.geocities.com/gibsonny5/
A Web site with teachers' resources, including primary source material, media library, lesson plans, and timelines.

www.nationalprojects.com/learningacademy/program_5.html
History site with movie excerpts.

www.usgennet.org/usa/topic/colonial/
An American local history network topic, including census records and timelines.

Source List

A selection of plays, movies, TV series, and musicals with Colonial American themes.

PLAYS AND MUSICALS

The Crucible (1954), by Arthur Miller

1776 (1969), by Peter Stone

MOVIES AND TV

The Adams Chronicles (1974), dir. various, with George Grizzard, William Daniels, Jeffrey Jones (TV miniseries)

The American Revolution (1994), dir. Lisa Bourgoujian, with Charles Durning, Kelsey Grammer, Michael Learned (TV documentary)

April Morning (1988), dir. Delbert Mann, with Tommy Lee Jones, Robert Urich, Chad Lowe

Benedict Arnold: A Question of Honor (2003), dir. Mikael Salomon, with Aidan Quinn, Kelsey Grammer, Flora Montgomery

The Bill of Rights (1939), dir. Crane Wilbur, with Ted Osborne, Moroni Olsen, Leonard Mudie

Black Robe (1991), dir. Bruce Beresford, with Lothaire Bluteau, Aden Young, Sandrine Holt

Colonial House (2004), dir. various (TV miniseries)

The Crossing (2000), dir. Robert Harmon, with Jeff Daniels, Roger Rees, Sebastian Roché

The Crucible (1957), dir. Raymond Rouleau, with Simone Signoret, Yves Montand, Mylène Demongeot

The Crucible (1996), dir. Nicholas Hytner, with Daniel Day-Lewis, Winona Ryder, Paul Scofield

Dear America: A Journey to the New World (1999), dir. Don McCutcheon, with Alison Pill, Andrew Airlie, Brenda Bazinet

Dear America: Standing in the Light (1999), dir. Stacey Stewart Curtis, with Marc Donato, Stephanie Mills, Grant Nickalls

Dear America: The Winter of Red Snow (1999), dir. Don McCutcheon, with Shawn Ashmore, Robert Bockstael, Conrad Coates

The Deerslayer (1978), dir. Richard Friedenberg, with Steve Forrest, Ned Romero, John Anderson

The Deserter (2003), dir. Eric Bruno Borgman, with Eric Bruno Borgman, Michael Kaplan, George Souza

Drums Along the Mohawk (1939), dir. John Ford, with Claudette Colbert, Henry Fonda, Edna May Oliver

Founding Brothers (2002), dir. various, with Brian Dennehy, Peter Coyote, Hal Holbrook (TV miniseries)

Founding Fathers (2000), dir. Mark Hufnail, Melissa Jo Peltier, with Brian Dennehy, Peter Coyote, Beau Bridges (TV miniseries)

George Washington (1984), dir. Buzz Kulik, with Barry Bostwick, Jaclyn Smith, Lloyd Bridges (TV miniseries)

George Washington II: The Forging of a Nation (1986), dir. William A. Graham, with Barry Bostwick, Patty Duke, Jeffrey Jones (TV miniseries)

The Howards of Virginia (1940), dir. Frank Lloyd, with Cary Grant, Martha Scott, Cedric Hardwicke

John Adams (2008), dir. Tom Hooper, with Paul Giamatti, Laura Linney, Stephen Dillane (TV miniseries)

Johnny Tremain (1957), dir. Robert Stevenson, with Hal Stalmaster, Luana Patten, Jeff York

The Last of the Mohicans (1936), dir. George B. Seitz, with Randolph Scott, Binnie Barnes, Bruce Cabot

The Last of the Mohicans (1991), dir. Michael Mann, with Daniel Day-Lewis, Madeleine Stowe, Russell Means

The New World (2005), dir. Terrence Malick, with Colin Farrell, Q'orianka Kilcher, Christopher Plummer

Northwest Passage (Book I—Rogers' Rangers) (1940), dir. King Vidor, with Spencer Tracy, Robert Young, Walter Brennan

The Patriot (2000), dir. Roland Emmerich, with Mel Gibson, Heath Ledger, Joely Richardson

Plymouth Adventure (1952), dir. Clarence Brown, with Spencer Tracy, Gene Tierney, Van Johnson

Pocahontas (1995), dir. Mike Gabriel, Eric Goldberg (Walt Disney animated feature)

The Rebels (1979), dir. Russ Mayberry, with Andrew Stevens, Don Johnson, Doug McClure

Revolution (1985), dir. Hugh Hudson, with Al Pacino, Donald Sutherland, Nastassja Kinski

The Scarlet Letter (1926), dir. Victor Sjostrom, with Lillian Gish, Lars Hanson, Karl Dane

The Scarlet Letter (1934), dir. Robert G. Vignola, with Colleen Moore, Hardie Albright, Henry B. Walthall

The Scarlet Letter (1995), dir. Roland Joffé, with Demi Moore, Gary Oldman, Robert Duvall

1776 (1972), dir. Peter Hunt, with Williams Daniel, Howard da Silva, Ken Howard

Sleepy Hollow (1999), dir. Tim Burton, with Johnny Depp, Christina Ricci, Miranda Richardson

Sons of Liberty (1939), dir. Michael Curtiz, with Claude Rains, Gale Sondergaard, Donald Crisp

Squanto: A Warrior's Tale (1994), dir. Xavier Koller, with Adam Beach, Sheldon Peters Wolfchild, Irene Bedard

Unconquered (1947), dir. Cecil B. de Mille, with Gary Cooper, Paulette Goddard, Boris Karloff

LIVING HISTORY MUSEUMS

Living history museums at Jamestown and Colonial Williamsburg in the United States stage historical re-enactments and exhibitions on permanent sites. At the Jamestown Settlement in Virginia, costumed historical interpreters guide visitors into the past, helping them try their hands at seventeenth-century activities. Colonial Williamsburg is the restored eighteenth-century capital of colonial Virginia. At Colonial Williamsburg, some costumed interpreters present their characters in the first person, and some give third-person interpretations. Visitors can rent costumes and play dress-up on a town-sized scale.

Index

Numbers in **bold** refer to illustrations.